The Life of a Sports Agent

To my beautiful fiancée, Jo, for your unconditional love and support of me and our gorgeous family. You live and breathe everything with me. Thank you and I love you with all my heart.

Also by Luke Sutton

Back from the Edge: Mental Health and Addiction in Sport (Pen & Sword, 2019)

The Life of a Sports Agent

The Middleman

Luke Sutton

WHITE OWL

AN IMPRINT OF PEN & SWORD BOOKS LTD.
YORKSHIRE - PHILADELPHIA

First published in Great Britain in 2020 by
Pen & Sword White Owl
An imprint of Pen & Sword Books Ltd
Yorkshire - Philadelphia

Copyright © Luke Sutton, 2020

ISBN 978 1 52673 699 4

The right of Luke Sutton to be identified as Author of this work has been asserted
by him in accordance with the Copyright, Designs and Patents Act 1988.

A CIP catalogue record for this book is available from the British Library.

Typeset in INDIA by IMPEC eSolutions
Printed and bound in England by TJ Books, Padstow, Cornwall

Pen & Sword Books Ltd. incorporates the Imprints of Pen & Sword Books
Archaeology, Atlas, Aviation, Battleground, Discovery, Family History,
History, Maritime, Military, Naval, Politics, Railways, Select, Transport,
True Crime, Fiction, Frontline Books, Leo Cooper, Praetorian Press,
Seaforth Publishing, Wharncliffe and White Owl.

For a complete list of Pen & Sword titles please contact:

PEN & SWORD BOOKS LIMITED
47 Church Street, Barnsley, South Yorkshire, S70 2AS, England
E-mail: enquiries@pen-and-sword.co.uk
Website: www.pen-and-sword.co.uk

or

PEN AND SWORD BOOKS
1950 Lawrence Rd, Havertown, PA 19083, USA
E-mail: uspen-and-sword@casematepublishers.com
Website: www.penandswordbooks.com

Contents

Introduction

I have been a sports agent for nearly a decade and almost any sporty guy I meet from a different walk of life says they would love to do what I do.

It always makes me think about the reality of what sports agents do – is it really that amazing? And why does everyone think it is so amazing? It can't all be down to Jerry Maguire!

We certainly have the fortune of walking with some sporting gods, and there is no question that that is truly magical. To be within the inner circle of a sporting genius and see what makes them tick, the hidden challenges they face, and then their performance in the sporting arena under the highest pressure, is nothing but the greatest privilege.

But what about everything in between? The things that other people don't really see? As I write this, I feel like I am giving this a negative connotation, but that's not necessarily true. There is much about being a sports agent that makes you believe there is nothing better to do in the world, other than playing sport yourself. But there is a lot involved.

Some really good and some really shit.

In essence, a sports agent is the ultimate middleman – in the middle of lots of people with lots of expectation and lots of potential conflict. You sit in between players and their families, clubs, sponsors, fans, media, coaches, managers, physios, financial advisers, friends, mortgage advisers, wives, husbands, girlfriends, boyfriends … the list goes on and on. You are in the middle of all these people, trying to manage their expectations, and at the same time having to find a way to enable your client, the player, to go out there and achieve everything possible from their career.

Your phone doesn't stop ringing and beeping, and you are the first person that people want to blame if it is too uncomfortable for them to blame each other, or themselves. Ever heard of the report from a football club that the agent was to blame for a falling-out with a player? Maybe the club and the player just fell out between themselves, but it was much more convenient to blame the agent. Ever heard of reports that an agent has been behaving immorally? Perhaps a player, a club or even a sponsor was behaving in that manner, but again, it is much easier the blame the agent.

You are the middleman – the first to be blamed and often the last to be praised. But you know what job you're in, so you can have no complaints. And, for all the pain, there are times that are so extraordinarily wonderful that they melt away all the troubles and allow you a moment of total euphoria.

So, over the next hundred pages or so, you will get an insight into what being a sports agent is actually like. I have seen the very best and the very worst that the industry offers, and you will read all about it here. I have been fortunate to manage athletes from many different sports, so I have a broad perspective of the industry. I have also been a player myself, so understand how elite athletes think and work.

Being a sports agent is wonderful. It is also very tough.

You are the ultimate middleman.

Chapter 1

Why We Need Agents

L et's face it; the reputation of sports agents is pretty poor. A friend of mine once told me that agents and tabloid gossip journalists are on a par, and I know a few journalists who would consider that an insult.

Gary Neville has enjoyed taking a swipe at football agents in the past:

> 'Footballers think they need agents – but it's not the case,'
> he said.

We've heard it from managers, chief executives, fans, your taxi driver, your golf partner etc. – agents are only interested in the money they take from people.

This well-trodden narrative has been selfishly used by people in sport to redirect reputational damage away from themselves. In this case we are specifically talking about football agents, but football is the barometer for the entire sports industry; and this discussion stretches across all sports.

I want to tackle this on a number of levels but let's start with the points made by Gary Neville. He called into question the use and regulation of football agents. To add some context to his statements, he was suggesting that footballers should take more responsibility for their representation and reach out to the Professional Footballers' Association – the players' union – and not independent agents, for help in this area.

Should players take more responsibility for their representation? I couldn't agree more. I actually think the cynicism towards agents is not all a bad thing. It makes parents and players look carefully at who they take on as an agent. Amen to that. Be careful and take responsibility for who you bring into your inner circle.

Regulation of agents? Absolutely, but the reality is that FIFA, as football's governing body, have battled for years to find an effective way to regulate the industry. If the global governing body are struggling to do this then regulation is going to be a challenge for the foreseeable future.

No use for independent agents? Total nonsense; and I will tell you why!

Gary Neville is rightly admired throughout the game. There are very few footballers or people from any walk of life as self-sufficient, intelligent, motivated and strong-minded as he is. There are also very few footballers who have stayed at the same club, or even just one other, for the whole of their career. Add to this that Gary played at Manchester United during a period of huge success. When you are laying the ground for potentially difficult contract talks, Gary's situation wouldn't have been at the top of the list. In fact, the greatest stress might have been when Sir Alex Ferguson asked him to stay on for another year when he felt he should retire. Even his brother's move from Manchester United to Everton is hardly one to use as an example of the norm. Phil wanted to leave United; the club respected that and wanted to help him move because he was such a loyal servant. They alerted other clubs and the deal was put in motion with Everton. But that is not a normal situation that we should judge the mechanics of the football industry by.

Ninety-nine point nine per cent of footballers are neither like Gary nor have his career. Some of them also don't have as strong a family around them as Gary has had throughout his career. So, the suggestion that all footballers should be more self-sufficient is asking things of people that they are just not capable of. That is not an excuse for them; it is a reality.

I'll come back to the point above, but let's handle another important part of Gary's argument. Firstly, players should only use the Professional Footballers' Association for representation – a body that was quite literally created to protect players. Makes sense, right? Unfortunately not. It is not a sustainable idea.

The PFA have some very good people working for them but they can't gather the resources to represent vast numbers of players, who range from the mediocre to the very best, and it is not possible to do this work without conflict.

In order to manage the very best players, you need to find the best agents with extensive commercial know-how and global football connections. Are these sorts of agents on the payroll of a players' union? Of course not. They are ambitious and go out on their own to make the sort of money their expertise can earn.

The PFA also need a good relationship with all football clubs. They work in partnership with them on various player initiatives and need the clubs' assistance in communicating with the players on a regular basis. I would suggest that the PFA would be less inclined to go into a hard-fought dispute with a club over a player's contract than an independent agent would be.

If you're not sure about that, ask why the very best players are not represented by the PFA.

If all of this is the case, then who should an 18-year-old potential superstar turn to for advice over his or her contract? A family member? In my nearly ten years of sports management, the biggest fuck-ups I have seen are without a doubt when a family member is representing a player. It almost always ends in disaster. That family member is often without experience or ability in the work required, and far too close to the player to give them a true third-party view on what is best for them. Sadly, that family member can also be a brother or father who is living their dreams through the player, which can be very unhealthy. The phrase I hear is, 'Let's keep the money in the family'. Trust me that money and relationships disappear mighty quickly when things get difficult. This is not always the situation but, in my experience, it is the sad truth in the vast majority of cases.

OK, so not a family member; well how about a lawyer, which is one of Gary's suggestions? For example, Roy Keane used his lawyer, Michael Kennedy, throughout his entire career.

This can definitely work: someone independent from the clubs and family, who understands the legal complexities of contracts, acting on your behalf. Absolutely great idea. But, guess what ... that lawyer is effectively an independent agent without much commercial experience within sport! Sure, the lawyer will have greater legal knowledge and experience, but any good agent will have a lawyer very close by in their operations to give them the necessary legal service.

The truth is that players shouldn't just get an agent for the sake of it, but if they do decide to get one, they should make sure they are good before hiring them. Common sense, really. You wouldn't hire a crap lawyer or accountant for the sake of it, either! But to twist this argument to question the use or value of an agent is something different, and a lazy analysis, in my opinion.

Players should take responsibility within their contract negotiations. They should stay informed and be involved in every decision. A good agent will encourage that. But the players are often very young, with little or zero experience of the real world. All they have done from a very early age is to be exceptional at a sport and be focused entirely on that. Schoolwork has often been left behind and they are unlikely to have ever worked in a 'proper job'. They might be very confident in their sphere of expertise but have little confidence in areas outside of that. If you ever need this proven, watch what happens when you bring a group of young professional sportsmen or women to a corporate function. They are often terrified, and stick together like glue. It's an environment they are just not used to. So expecting them to take a lead on something that can be as confrontational and complicated as a contract negotiation is completely unrealistic.

While we are here, let's talk through the work of Paul Pogba's agent, Mino Raiola – a man who has been much maligned over the years. Raiola is infamous for his handling of Pogba and has been widely criticised by numerous people within the football world. He has not been shy to use his mouth and has been referred to as an agent 'out of control'. Sir Alex Ferguson allegedly described him as a 'bad agent' and a 'shitbag'. Really? Why don't we have a closer look at this …

Paul Pogba was a highly talented and ambitious teenage footballer at Manchester United in 2012. Sir Alex wanted Pogba to sign a new contract to keep him at the club. Pogba wanted to play more first team football. In Raiola's eyes, the contract offered was unacceptable, but also, Pogba's personal ambitions were not being met at the club. They turned down the contract offer and left. Granted, it was perhaps declined in a manner that was not entirely respectful!

To this day, Sir Alex still wants to make this about money. He says that United offered Pogba an amazing contract, and he and his agent were greedy and wanted more. Yes, money is important, it is to everyone, but the best young players want to play, and that's the most important thing. If a manager wants to keep a player but knows that doing so will hold them back slightly, who is the one acting in the best interests of the player?

Raiola rightly challenged Sir Alex – the most successful manager for generations and a god at Manchester United – because he knew it was right for Pogba. Sir Alex didn't like being so openly challenged or the fact that he was going to lose this highly talented young player.

Pogba walked away from the biggest club in the world. Can you imagine the trust that must have existed between Pogba and Raiola? Incredible. Pogba trusted that he was doing the right thing in challenging the greatest football manager in the world. They went to Juventus, where Pogba played a huge role in the success of that team, eventually helping them to a UEFA Champions League Final in 2015.

If only Sir Alex had still been at Manchester United when the deal was done to buy Pogba back for a world-record transfer of £89 million! It was also reported that Raiola made a fortune from the deal himself. In fact, on hearing Sir Alex's criticism of him, Raiola said, 'Those words don't describe my work in a negative way. I rate them as a proof that I am good at my job.'

I want to add more to the point I am making about the Pogba/ Raiola situation. Pogba is now a huge adidas asset, having signed a multi-million-pound deal with them in the build-up to him joining Manchester United. While Pogba was at Juventus, every major football brand was chasing his signature, and for years, he and Raiola resisted committing him to anyone long-term. One match he would wear Nike boots, the next it would be Pumas, and then adidas ... Many people thought it was an odd play as Pogba was missing out on a lucrative boot and apparel deal by not committing to anyone. But Raiola stood firm and told him not to until someone got to the number that he believed was possible. Raiola wanted an eight-figure contract for Pogba and believed it would come eventually. Again, imagine the trust between Pogba and Raiola for him to accept missing out on boot contracts in a bid to wait for the big one. It's extraordinary, and makes the whole story behind them even more incredible.

Raiola secures Pogba's dream move back to Manchester United and in turn secures him a huge endorsement deal with adidas. Whether we like the way in which he works and communicates or not, I think it would be inaccurate to describe Mino Raiola as a 'bad agent'.

* * *

I expect that many of you have never heard the point of view I have just given on how agents are misrepresented by people within the sports industry. Now don't for one minute believe that I don't think that there are some incapable and corrupt agents out there. Of course there are, and that's why I wholeheartedly support greater regulation of the industry. But there are incapable and corrupt people in all sorts of positions within the sports world; and that's because money breeds corruption. That's true in every walk of life. People with power and money want to keep it and people without power and money want to get it.

I recently heard the ex-Crystal Palace owner, Simon Jordan, describe agents as 'parasitical little turds' who are 'the basis of every aspect of corruption within the business of football'. This is just straight-up lazy analysis. There are some poor and corrupt agents, just like there are football club owners. To focus corruption solely on agents says more about him than it does about agents. I suspect Simon feels some bitterness to how his ownership of Crystal Palace ended up, and rather than look at the mistakes he made, will find agents an easy target.

So, as I said earlier, in the middle of everything is the agent. The middleman.

We provide the perfect foil for someone to blame. The punchbag if something goes wrong.

Without agents, the sports industry would grind to a halt. But try to find someone to tell you that and I'll give you a pretty penny. One of the most lauded sets of figures released each year is how much football clubs have paid agents in that season. Everyone is horrified and immediately talks about how much money is 'leaving the game' and that something needs to change. And guess what; nothing changes, because it can't. Without agents, the whole football industry doesn't work.

Why is so much attention given to how much agents earn? And why is it always spun in a negative light? Imagine a world in which agents were praised for giving fluidity to the industry and helping to avoid constant conflict between everyone. Now that would be something!

So maybe it is just to distract from some awkward questions over players' wages, executives' wages, ticket prices, merchandise prices, increasing levels of broadcasting rights and vast debts being run up by sporting clubs?

Football is the workingman's game but the connection between that demographic and what runs the game was blurred a long time ago. The heart of the sport has been lost.

A couple of years ago, I received a letter from a mother in Liverpool begging me to arrange a time for her 5-year-old son to meet my client, Simon Mignolet, who was at Liverpool FC at the time. It was a beautifully written letter and I showed it to Simon, who is hands down one of the most intelligent and nicest footballers you will ever meet. Simon asked me to arrange a time for the boy and his mum to come into Melwood, Liverpool's training ground, to meet him.

I met them in reception at Melwood and the boy could not stop talking. He was beyond excited about meeting Simon. He had brought with him his full home and away kit, plus his boots, to be signed. The mother was in tears at the opportunity and couldn't thank me enough. Simon came down after training and it was an amazing thirty minutes. It is what football should be all about – a boy or girl being inspired by their idol to do as much as they can with their life.

As it all died down and Simon said his goodbyes, I chatted more to the mother about whether they were going to the game at the weekend. She told me they would do their best, but it would depend on what she could earn this week and what they could get the tickets off the touts for. She reckoned she could get one ticket for £200 and would look for a pair: £400 for a single parent who could barely make ends meet, and yet she talked about it like it was her duty to fulfil. Something was very wrong with this.

I'm not trying to pretend agents are holier than thou and deserving of lavish praise. Greed and corruption have infiltrated agents as much as they have in any area of sport. But we are also targets for unnecessary blame within the industry.

When we sit down with a 17-year-old boy or girl on the edge of a career that could change their family's life, I know I have a great responsibility and I respect that. I take my job seriously and I know that I'm good at it. I know I operate in an area of huge risk. If something goes well, it is to the player's or club's credit, but when something goes wrong, it is my fault. I expect to be paid well for my work, and that's not unreasonable.

There is a lot that sport needs to fix.

Agents should not be top of that list.

Chapter 2

Jimmy Anderson

J immy Anderson definitely felt like a brother to me in many ways. We sat next to each other in the dressing room when I was at Lancashire CCC and seemed to hit it off almost immediately. You could argue that this was mainly because he enjoyed relentlessly taking the piss out of my relatively posh accent! The character 'Ziggy', who was in the Big Brother house that previous winter, didn't help my cause at all; he also had a posh accent and a similar long-haired look. It was actually very rare that Jimmy would talk to me in his natural Burnley accent.

I really liked Jimmy from the off. He was introverted, intelligent and very funny. There always seemed much more to him than people thought. He could be a bit awkward at times, but I quite liked that rather than someone being too overbearing.

Jimmy was actually at a bit of a crossroads in his career at the time. It was 2005, and he was recovering from his major back injury and had yet to fully establish himself in the England team. He was definitely not the polished performer we eventually knew him to be. He had also just got married to Daniella, who similarly became like a sister to me. I really liked the both of them. During the toughest times of my personal problems, I leant on them a lot and they were always there for me.

I managed Jimmy entirely for the best part of six years, from 2011 to 2017. It was roughly the period that covered Jimmy taking 200 Test wickets to just over 500 Test wickets.

Jimmy is unquestionably a sporting genius. He was my first client and I learned more about myself and athlete management from managing him than from anything else.

* * *

I actually never wanted to venture into sports management. I didn't have a great regard for the industry, bar one or two excellent agents I had met, but I worried it might compromise the rest of my business. Activate Management operated solely as a sports and activity coaching business in 2011, and we already worked with a number of high-profile athletes, so I didn't want our position to come into question.

However, Jimmy was struggling with his management at the time so we started talking about whether it was something I could help with. I had a sense that I thought we could be good at it because we knew the commercial world, we knew what elite players needed and, crucially, I knew Jimmy really well. After a lot of thought on both sides, we decided to go for it.

In my opinion, Jimmy was not being maximised either on or off the field – a handsome man with intelligence and creativity, who just needed to find his platforms to express himself, which he didn't find easy. For many introverted people, they can be hugely creative but find it tough to express that creativity. That was exactly Jimmy. In some aspects of life, he burst with confidence, but in others, he needed a lot of reassurance. I sometimes watch how polished he now sounds on radio and TV and remember the early days – he has come a long way! Even though he was one of my best friends, objectively I always felt that Jimmy had enormous potential to do much more with his career in cricket and beyond.

In my early days of managing Jimmy, it was about finding ways to raise his profile and commercial worth without asking him to do things that he would find uncomfortable. It was a really tough balance. Jimmy is a master of his trade, obviously, so although he wanted to do more off the field, it needed to be balanced with what he liked and not interfere with his cricket. That is the ultimate challenge of athlete management.

An example of where I believed we made it work, in 2012, Jimmy had a newspaper column with the *Mail on Sunday*, which was ghostwritten by the excellent Peter Hayter. This was an opportunity for us to raise Jimmy's profile off the field. In fact, 2012 was the perfect time for this.

Jimmy always had opinions. The newspaper, by nature, was keen to make an impression, and this was a spectacularly controversial time for the England cricket team. Kevin Pietersen was in full flow as a player but also were the tensions between him, the ECB and the rest of the team, with everything eventually blowing up over the scandal that he had been texting the opposition at the time, South Africa, about the England captain, Andrew Strauss.

We took some risks with how far we pushed that column, and at times Jimmy said much more than other players. But by doing it in a newspaper, we had control of the wording and Jimmy didn't feel the pressure of having to express himself in front of a camera or microphone. It was a really good platform for him to do this. So, by putting his head above the parapet, Jimmy risked criticisms and analysis, which he got; but he also became noticeable. We combined this with getting Jimmy featured in more TV and radio shows and magazines that were outside of the cricket bubble. We pushed forward Jimmy's interest in music, fashion and film to try to take his profile beyond the traditional circles. It certainly helped that he signed a sponsorship deal with Wellman/Vitabiotics at the end of 2011, which meant his advert was plastered all over London buses and the Tube. Jimmy was gathering momentum on the field but now there was also something building for him off the field. His profile was growing beyond the traditional cricket fan base.

But make no mistake, over the course of time my job was made exponentially easier because Jimmy is a pure genius as far as his cricket is concerned. He was always able to back up whatever work we did for him outside of cricket with extraordinary performances on the field. There were countless occasions where he reminded me what a genius he was. I would imagine that people would point towards the record-breaking moments, but it is not those moments that stand out most for me. In fact, I have two distinctive, if perhaps a little offbeat, memories that helped me understand why Jimmy is Jimmy.

The first is from the England tour to the West Indies in 2015, when Jimmy was on the brink of breaking Sir Ian Botham's long-held record for the most number of Test wickets for an Englishman. Jimmy was only four wickets away from breaking the record, and the First Test in Antigua was the one where it looked like it was going to happen. I had actually mapped this match as being the record-breaking one about six months previously. I was tracking how fast Jimmy was taking wickets and worked out that this was most likely the Test in which it he would achieve it. As a result, a large group of friends and family came out, and suddenly, I felt an enormous amount of pressure for having made this prediction! I also worried about the pressure it would place on Jimmy, but, as always, he handled it magnificently. After a little bit of a struggle on a dead pitch, the moment came when he found the edge of Denesh Ramdin's bat, and Alastair Cook did the rest at first slip. It was an historic occasion for Jimmy and English cricket. The baton of greatness was being handed from Botham to Anderson. It was an amazing milestone.

But this wasn't the moment that Jimmy's genius hit home for me.

It was actually in the Second Test match in Grenada. Bar me and Jimmy's mum and dad, the group of friends and family went home after Antigua. I stayed on just in case he took one more Test than I had predicted to break the record. After Antigua, Jimmy was exhausted. He had bowled forty-seven overs and had had the enormous high of breaking the record as well as the celebrations that came afterwards. So, when he arrived in Grenada, he was tired. Really tired. And I think we could all excuse him for that. England then bowled first on a wicket that was doing a bit for the bowlers but was extremely slow. They bowled OK on day one, but the game was very much in the balance as England struggled to dominate a gutsy West Indian side led by a brilliant hundred from Marlon Samuels. The match meandered to the morning of day five as England struggled to take wickets, with a hundred from Kraigg Brathwaite on a lifeless and slow pitch. Exactly the sort of wicket that critics of Jimmy would say that there was nothing in it for him. Yet on the morning of day five he produced a spell of bowling that entirely turned the Test match around. He raised his pace to the high 80s mph and found life in a pitch that everyone else was struggling with. He blew the West Indians away with 4/43 and England won the Test. It might seem an odd moment for me to pick out as to why Jimmy is a genius, but for me, it isn't. It summed up perfectly why Jimmy is above all others. There was every reason why Jimmy could have had a quiet match in Grenada, and no one would have blamed him. No one at all. There was a window that could have allowed him to mentally turn it down a notch, but he didn't do that. In fact, he did the absolute opposite and raised his intensity to win the Test match for England. That is what greats do. They don't dwell on a record-breaking moment; they move on and approach the next match with exactly the same amount of intensity.

The second moment that stands out for me is also a bit different from what you might imagine. During 2016, Jimmy had been carrying a shoulder injury, and eventually it proved too much and he had to have some time out. This meant that he didn't go in the original squad on the tour of India that October. An India tour is always brutal for a fast bowler, and again, this was a time when Jimmy could have been excused for stepping back. His shoulder needed resting and he could have had a longer rehab to avoid the tough conditions out there. So, what did Jimmy do? The absolute opposite. He fought tooth and nail to get fit and then prove his fitness to get out there as soon as he could. There were very few people left in England at that time of the year to help Jimmy prove his fitness to the England management. Almost all county players were having an end-of-season break or had already gone overseas. As a result, Jimmy popped the question to me: 'I don't suppose you fancy having a bat in the nets against me?'

I hadn't batted for five years and I had no kit, but this was not a time to say 'no' to England's all-time greatest bowler. Jimmy wanted to film himself bowling in the nets to show the England management how well he was doing. He was desperate to get out on the tour, despite not having played a competitive match for several weeks. With regards to the net session – well, I walked in wondering if this would be the moment that I had dreamt of, where everything clicked, and I batted with elegance, power and grace; a mixture of Viv Richards and Sachin Tendulkar. I just let myself believe that after a five-year break, this would be it; it would all come good and the great Jimmy Anderson would be taken down …

Yeah, that didn't happen. I mishit the first bowl and after that I got more and more crablike in a desperate battle to get something behind the ball. He was great, and I was even more average than when I had stopped playing five years previously.

Anyway, the point was that Jimmy, in the quiet of the Old Trafford Indoor Cricket Centre, was showing why he was a true great of the game. His mentality was extraordinary. He literally had nothing to prove going on this tour and yet he was going above and beyond to get there. Very few people saw this part of Jimmy, but that is why, in my eyes, he is peerless. He has crafted wonderful skills with the ball, but above all else, his mentality to perform and compete went far and beyond that of others. That is why he has now played over 150 Test matches and taken more wickets than anyone else. Incidentally, he did get himself out to India, playing in the Second Test match and bowling thirty-five overs and taking four wickets. An incredible effort by him, and why he is a champion.

* * *

I am sure Jimmy would still have had a wonderful career without my help because of his ability to perform at the highest of levels. Nonetheless, I'm sure we gave him a sense of comfort in a number of ways that helped him. On this point – always beware of an agent claiming credit for their client's on-field success. If someone wants to get the credit, then they should absolutely take the blame when things don't go well. However, that type of agent is rarely seen when it all starts to go wrong!

A funny story that taught me this lesson was when Jimmy toured India in the winter of 2012. England were going through the warm-up games for this much-anticipated and hugely challenging series for England. I got a message from Jimmy:

'Mate, I need you to find me some extra-long spikes. I can't stand up at the crease with the ground over here. It's an absolute nightmare.'

Eager to help, and loving a challenge, I was all over this. The first Test was less than two weeks away. Just call me Anneka Rice!

'No worries, mate, I'm on it.'

Jimmy was sponsored by adidas, so I called them to enquire if they had any – no. I researched online and called all my contacts at UK cricket brands and shops: no one had any. No one made them anymore! In my mind, England's hopes in India entirely rested on whether I could find these bloody long spikes and get them to Jimmy – OK, a bit dramatic, but you know what I mean.

My search had to go global and I eventually found a shop in Brisbane, Australia, who had some. And who owned that shop? Joe Dawes, the newly appointed bowling coach for the Indian Cricket Team! The contact number I found online was actually Joe's mobile number, so I called him, and we had this rather awkward conversation, with me desperately begging him to help me and explaining the urgency of the whole situation.

Joe had the spikes, but we now had to work out how to get them from Brisbane to Mumbai in time for the First Test. Taking into account Indian customs and the reliability of the postal service out there, this was a total nightmare. I actually went back to Jimmy at this stage and said we might not be able to do it, and he replied: 'I need them, mate, otherwise I can't stand up at the crease.'

This was desperate. Jimmy needed me. England cricket needed me. Just call me bloody Superman.

I was not giving up.

I made some panicky calls to the ECB to find out if any staff or officials were going out shortly before the First Test and discovered Ashley Giles was my man. But now we had a race against time to get the spikes from Brisbane to Birmingham in time for Ashley's flight. I pestered Joe relentlessly about whether he had posted them and if it had been done correctly. I was incredibly annoying, and he was incredibly patient, especially considering he was working for the opposition!

I tracked the spikes leaving Brisbane and being flown over to the UK. All was OK.

I had then organised a motorbike courier to pick them up from the UK depot and take them immediately to Ashley, who was about to get on his flight. I tracked the motorbike. All was OK.

Ashley got the spikes ... and got on his flight ... and got them to Jimmy. ALL WAS OK!

To this day, it is in my top three achievements in sports management. A logistical nightmare that could have fallen apart by one small detail not working.

I sat back and watched the series in India unfold. Jimmy was unbelievable. His performance throughout the series crushed the theory that he could only bowl in England and he was elevated to a new status in world cricket. England won the series 2-1 and India's captain, MS Dhoni, pinpointed Jimmy as being the difference between the two sides.

This was a huge result for England, and for Jimmy. It was an incredibly difficult place to succeed and they had triumphed emphatically.

And ...

I have to admit, I felt a large dose of credit for this. Without those spikes, Jimmy would not have been able to perform as he did. A seminal moment in England's cricket history. I had saved the day – OK, again dramatic, but let's just run with my ego at the time.

As soon as Jimmy landed back in England, I arranged a lunch catch-up with him. We met at Piccolino's in Hale, and I will admit I was waiting for that declaration of: 'Fucking hell, Luke, without you, that might not have been possible.'

Anyway, nothing like that came out in the conversation, but we were both in high spirits, so I said, 'So, how about those spikes, mate? Were they great for you? I am so happy I managed to get them to you.'

As if he was commenting on the weather, Jimmy flippantly replied, 'Nah, mate. Didn't bother using them in end.'

WHAT?

Lesson learned.

* * *

In the end, Jimmy and I began bringing our working relationship to an end towards the end of the summer of 2017. I'm not too proud to say that I found it really hard to deal with.

I had always thought Jimmy and I were forever – above all else, we would always work together. So, when I realised that he wanted to move on to something else, I didn't quite know how to react. I found the next few months tough. I was heartbroken, to be honest, and it took me a long time to come to terms with it. I watched Jimmy take his 500th Test wicket at Lord's on television, and I cried. I was officially managing him then, but we were already in the process of the split. It was such a pinnacle in his career and I always envisaged sharing the joy of that moment with him and his family. But everything had changed.

Even our management separation was tricky to sort. I was intricately woven into Jimmy's life, so it was never going to take just a couple of emails. A bit like a divorce, I guess. I knew it was hard for Jimmy to do what he was doing. I was his mate, godfather to his daughter, his right-hand man for so long; this was a huge thing for him too.

However, as I said at the start of this chapter, I learned so much about myself from managing Jimmy and, after some time, I have been able to put all of this into perspective.

The most important thing I would say is that Jimmy making that decision was absolutely the right thing to do – definitely for him at the time, and also, eventually, for me.

Our relationship or, more importantly, my management of him, had been all-encompassing. I controlled everything in his life, but I don't think I let him breathe. During all this time, he was developing as a person and I was still treating him like a teenager who needed to listen to me all the time. I wasn't empowering him to drive his own direction.

I had also started to take the relationship for granted. The belief in my head that our professional association was forever was a dangerous one. I don't believe it was the case that my work was any less productive, but maybe I wasn't taking as long to listen to where he was at. He was coming towards the end of his career and I was just rushing around expecting him to follow me.

So, now, I totally understand why we needed to go our separate ways. For him, it was to find his own path and see what that was like, and for me, it was to put myself in check and allow myself to learn and grow from the experience.

I now realise that as I manage young players and watch them develop, I need to remember to allow them to take ownership of their direction. I am there to advise and assist, not to entirely control. It is not my career; it is theirs. Thinking I know better is really dangerous, and can lead to a nasty bump along the way … as happened to me.

I was very fortunate to manage England's greatest-ever bowler throughout the crucial years of his career. I think I did a decent job but, most importantly, I came away from it learning so much about myself and how I need to handle myself going forward.

More importantly, Jimmy and I will always be friends.

Chapter 3

Working with the Media

The relationship between a sports agent and the media is a really interesting one. Ultimately, we need each other.

The power of social media has made this whole dynamic even more complex and necessary.

There can be an attitude amongst some agents or players along the lines of, 'Don't speak to the media, you can't trust them!' My attitude is the complete opposite of that.

As an agent, you should almost always be under the radar. But to the media, you can't be invisible. You need to build relationships with as many journalists as you can and, if they know their job, they will be doing the same with you. I give my mobile number freely to journalists and encourage them to call me anytime.

Journalists have to write something. It's their job and they should be respected for it. Sports journalists are decent people reporting on their relevant sport specialism. We might not always agree with their opinion, but they are just doing their job.

So, if journalists need to write up good content, in whatever format, why wouldn't someone like me keep an open but sensible line of communication with them? This is not about trying to get them to write something; a match or performance is what it is, after all! This is about making sure they have all the information they need to have a balanced view on whatever they are writing about. Journalists will never not want more information or context. Sometimes they will seek it from me and sometimes I will offer it. This isn't about leaking confidential information; this is about developing a healthy relationship with the media. This doesn't just hold with the written media; it is the same with TV and radio broadcasters.

In my opinion, if you don't engage with the media then you have little room to complain if they report something inaccurately.

* * *

Simon Mignolet has been a client of mine for a number of years and while at Liverpool FC was, at times, subject to brutal media attention. Simon is a ten-out-of-ten professional and a lovely and intelligent man. The avalanche of negativity directed at him was sometimes very unfair. He made some mistakes in matches, but generally, his performances were very consistent. His mistakes were blown up by the likes of Gary Neville and Jamie Carragher, although not because I think they had a specific agenda against Simon. Gary has always been very critical of goalkeepers, and being Liverpool's goalkeeper would mean you would be under the most intense spotlight from him. In Jamie's case, I believe he genuinely felt Liverpool needed to recruit a new goalkeeper and in his frustration that they didn't, he would on occasion boil over into overtly intense criticism of Simon. I managed Simon's Twitter account for a period of time and the trolling was horrific. A so-called 'fan' tweeted him an image of him being shot in a firing squad line-up. Simon still had access to his account, and I prayed he didn't look at it. I'm certainly not blaming Gary Neville or Jamie Carragher for this; they were just doing their jobs, but the spillover was this sort of thing.

Simon and I discussed it a lot during the last two or three years of his time at Liverpool and I worked actively to try to help him with this. I engaged the football media as well as I could, but the best place for us to start was his social media. Combined across Twitter, Instagram and Facebook, Simon had millions of followers, so here we had a place to show people what Simon was really like, rather than be positioned as some lame duck that people could take a pot-shot at.

We engaged an external company to help us with this and identified the key aspects to Simon's personality on which to focus:

he was a brilliant professional
he was a top Premier League goalkeeper
he was loyal
he was a family man
he was intelligent
he had a sense of humour.

A whole social media strategy was written up that Simon led and everyone bought into. Every single post involved planning and consultation with Simon. We were sensitive to timings and always kept close to the key points that we were trying to remind fans about concerning Simon's personality. I have to say, it was a massive success.

Simon's engagement on social media increased enormously but, most importantly, fans started to see his true personality. We weren't painting a picture that wasn't true; it was absolutely a true reflection of Simon, but up to that point, the truth was being swamped by this avalanche of negativity towards him. Fans began to appreciate Simon for who and what he was. Yes, he had made some mistakes, but suddenly they weren't overshadowing everything he offered as a person and a player to Liverpool FC. I felt really proud when I saw fans joining the likes of James Milner and Jürgen Klopp on commenting about what an incredible professional he was in and around Liverpool winning the Champions League in 2019.

We backed up the social media work with the odd interview in the mainstream media to help consolidate all of this. It really did work, and when Simon left Liverpool at the end of summer 2019 for Club Brugge, the mutual respect between him, the fans and the club was excellent. It was how it should have been. It wasn't about creating lies; it was about trying to balance things so that Simon was treated fairly by everyone.

There are times with my work when the small, unnoticed things are the things you are most proud of.

This was most definitely one of them.

* * *

In the last ten years, the England cricket team has appeared to have attracted a disproportionate number of headlines to any other of our national teams. There have been the various fallings-out with Kevin Pietersen and, of course, the more recent Ben Stokes' late-night brawl outside a nightclub in Bristol.

I actually believe that the Kevin Pietersen falling-out with the ECB was a watershed for many in the sports industry over how to handle such situations with the media. The rights and wrongs of Kevin Pietersen as a person don't really interest me, and whether his ousting was the correct decision is widely subjective. What was far more interesting to me was how it played out in the public domain.

We witnessed, at the time, a traditional governing body in the ECB trying to deal with a rogue individual who was very strong on social media and, importantly, had supporters even stronger online.

KP's army, led by Piers Morgan, waged war on Twitter. Piers & Co. ferociously attacked anyone remotely anti-KP. It was brutal and ugly. The ECB stood still – likely shocked and conning themselves that if they said nothing it would eventually all blow over. They were briefing the media behind the scenes on his misdemeanours and believing that was enough. But KP and Piers were dominating in the exact online space that the majority of the game's younger fans were consuming their media from.

Yet the ECB continued to bury their heads in the sand. In the face of brutal personal attacks on the England captain, Alastair Cook, little was done to try to counter this. Players were left isolated and terrified that they would be next in the barrel of KP's supporters online. At that time the ECB were light years behind, with no answer. It was embarrassing. A bloodbath … online. Thankfully, the new leadership at the ECB, who took over after this, recognised the mistakes and now get on the front foot when it comes to the online space.

I remember thinking that there were important lessons for the whole sports industry, including agents, to learn here. The PR battlefield lands online and everything else follows. It was all well and good me having decent relationships with journalists, but sports people's social media accounts were the most powerful tool to control their PR.

The message to all clients ten years ago was very much 'don't say anything stupid on social media'. Of course, that still applies today, but back then it meant that the human side of athletes began to be eroded from their social media feeds. It was like listening to and watching the most boring media-trained athlete online. Everything was ridiculously safe.

KP's situation taught me that the clever ones amongst us will use social media to get ahead of the game. Fill that media space with what you want. Encourage clients to show their human side and not just post the usual clichéd crap. Yes, it comes with risks, but it also comes with great benefits, so it is a risk worth taking, in my opinion.

The millennial generation are consuming media and forming their opinion first and foremost online. For sports people, social media represents an opportunity to engage with fans and control their own PR.

The agents who are still terrified by the media, in general, are likely to be the ones playing it completely safe on social media. My attitude is very different. We should engage with it all and get on the front foot.

* * *

The one client I wished I could have helped more in the media was Peter Moores.

There is not a better man in cricket than Peter. A brilliant coach and a really good person. Fundamentally, he just wanted the best for every single player he worked with. It sounds simple, but often coaches come with egos or their own agendas to build their reputations. Peter doesn't have an ounce of that. It is why the vast majority of players absolutely love working with him. He has 100 per cent integrity.

Peter might have made some mistakes in his approach as an England coach the first time around but, much like Simon Mignolet, the avalanche of negativity that bulldozed him created a false impression.

In 2015, Peter was sacked for the second time by the ECB as England's head coach. This was at a time when Andrew Strauss took over as supremo of England cricket, but also in the aftermath of Peter being horrendously misquoted after England disastrously crashed out of the 2015 World Cup when they lost to Bangladesh.

Peter was heavily criticised after appearing to say 'we will look at the data' following the loss to Bangladesh, which was, in actual fact, an incorrect transcription of the interview he did with the BBC's *Test Match Special*. In actual fact, 'will we look at the data' was misheard for 'we will look at that later'. He was eventually sent an official apology letter from the BBC following the incorrect transcription – but the damage was done. Peter was labelled as some sort of data-driven, robot-styled coach. It couldn't have been further from the truth. In fact, the only time Peter mentioned data in the media was when he said, 'Now is not the time to look at data.'

Social media immediately, and with an unstoppable force, amplified the misquotation. Before anyone could do anything, it was everywhere. Alison Mitchell, the interviewer at the time, did try to correct this on her own social media soon afterwards, but the public were baying for blood after such poor performances, and Peter was the perfect fall guy.

All of this deeply hurt Peter and his family. He is a proud man and they are a very close and loving unit. There was really nothing they could do at that time other than to let the storm settle down and then try to address it. But it was incredibly hard on them. I was there to support them and find solutions, but the main difficulty was that no one really wanted to sympathise with Peter. Fans and journalists alike were annoyed at England's performance, so whether it was accurate or not, they all seemed to want to blame Peter. Now Peter wasn't ever on social media, so he had little or no means of reply. He just had to get on with his job and hope that, in time, people would move on.

After his sacking, we lined up a couple of interviews with ESPNcricinfo and the *Daily Mail*. Both were excellent interviews, in which Peter gave an honest reflection on his sacking and everything that had happened after the World Cup. The interviews were well received. However, I watched Sky Sports that night with the cricket highlights show presented by Charles Colvile, and during the show, he said something along the lines of: 'I see Peter Moores has done a couple of interviews and is now blaming the press for his sacking.'

What utter rubbish from Charles.

Peter gave two honest, humble and graceful interviews. He was rightly hurt by what happened with the misquotation, which I think any of us, including Charles, would have been. He wasn't blaming anyone for his sacking, but the negativity around him had certainly not been helped by that misquote. He handled the whole affair with more integrity that many of us could ever muster, and yet Charles just took another cheap shot at him, and in doing so, highlighted exactly why Peter was poorly treated during that time. Charles didn't think twice about making that comment and probably didn't give it a thought afterwards, yet Peter battled against this sort of negativity for years.

Charles wasn't 'doing his job' in that moment; he was playing to a crowd who still felt massive disappointment after the World Cup performance. In my opinion, quality sports broadcasting is not about playing to the crowd.

I felt unable to help Peter in this situation and it was a horrible feeling. He was as good a man as any in cricket, and I couldn't shift the tide for him. He deserved better. It highlighted for me, once again, how social media can be such a powerful platform in allowing you to have some control of headlines and perception. Peter wasn't on social media and England head coaches at the time were encouraged to stay under the radar, but it meant Peter had no ability to get on the front foot.

It is probably why I reacted so badly on the day Peter was sacked for the second time. England were playing Ireland in a One-Day International and reports were breaking all over the media that Peter was due to be sacked. It seemed everyone knew except for Peter, who was coaching England in this game. This leak of information turned out to be true, but, regardless, was extremely poor. Peter had only ever handled himself with total professionalism and grace, yet time and time again, he was treated poorly by people who should have known better. This leak summed the whole thing up for me.

I couldn't help myself as my frustration boiled over and I fired off a few angry tweets, which I would tell any client not to do! I was desperately trying to get hold of key people at the England and Wales Cricket Board to find out if this was true and, as I struggled to get any real information, I just felt it was another cruel blow for Peter.

I deleted my tweets but obviously a few national newspapers had already screenshot them and they were used in the next day's reporting. I don't particularly regret it as someone needed to say something, but I always feel that agents should just keep their heads down, and this time I was doing the absolute opposite.

Over the years I have learned so much about handling the media, including the online space. The biggest lesson the Peter Moores scenario taught me was that every client should be on social media. No exceptions. Get onto the front foot. Be sensible and have a clear strategy, but don't leave that space open for other people to fill with nonsense.

* * *

I will dedicate an entire chapter on how social media now dominates my work and how the sports industry has been slow but now very effective in maximising it for gain. However, before I do that, I would like to end this chapter by making a point about how high-profile athletes or coaches should view the dynamic of social media.

Put very simply, the ones who understand it make their social media channels a two-way conversation between them and fans; the ones who are lost in their own self-importance believe it is about them telling the world what they think is important, and that's it. By nature, social media is about the masses following singular, high-profile people because they admire them, are intrigued by them or even hate them; but the conversation doesn't have to – and, in fact, shouldn't – be like that.

The best analogy I can give is that an athlete putting out a tweet and then not engaging with any of the replies is much like reading out a statement at a press conference and then not taking any questions before walking out. It might feel easier to do that, but it won't win you any admirers, and your authenticity will be questioned. This was exactly how people used social media five years or so ago, because they believed it was safe; but it was a mistake.

The biggest of stars might be able to get away with this, but not many others. For 99 per cent of the sporting world, they must view their social media as their community, and it will contain both love and hate. It is important to allow fans to feel part of what you are posting, and encourage them to chat to you. Make them feel like they are welcome, and not like you are sitting on top of some sort of pedestal. I encourage clients to reply to people and to 'like' or repost things. Of course, you need to be as sensible as you would be in a press conference if you are attacked or asked a silly question; but, by all means, engage!

Social media has for too long been measured on the number of followers or subscribers; now, more than anything else, it is measured on engagement. If you are an athlete and want to build your fan base and your commercial off-field earnings, then create engaging two-way social media channels. The rest will follow for you!

People have generally been slow to understand the power of social media and it will continue to evolve, but the major players in the sports industry, whether they are players, teams, brands, organisations or agents, are ahead of the game on this front.

Chapter 4

Sam Quek

I t had been a matter of days since the closing ceremony of the 2016 Olympic Games in Rio de Janeiro and Team GB had returned triumphantly with their best medal haul ever. My phone rang:

'Hi Luke, my name is Thomas Mairs and I am Sam Quek's partner. We have been recommended you and would like to talk to you about possibly managing Sam.'

That still makes me laugh because it is the only time Tom has ever called himself 'Thomas' to me!

Like millions of other people in the UK, I had followed the incredible run of the GB Women's Hockey team all the way to their wonderful gold medal win live on BBC1. The girls had absolutely caught the imagination of the nation and the final was the most dramatic climax to it all. Of course, Maddie Hinch took the majority of the headlines after the final but I had noticed Sam throughout the tournament as well as in the final.

Once upon a time, I had been a keen hockey player at Millfield School so knew 'a bit' about the game. Sam was certainly one of the stand-out players of the tournament and I loved the way she recovered from an early mistake in the final to finish the match strongly. Looking from the outside, she seemed to have real character and spirit. She was very good looking, which, of course, added to her standing out from the others. I had seen a photo shoot that Sam did pre-tournament that was a little edgy and showed that she was incredibly photogenic. She seemed to have everything to make her a star, and I certainly knew who she was.

As the call came through, I was in the Renaissance Hotel at St Pancras in London, and the phone reception was terrible. I was desperate to hear Tom clearly but was battling away with the line.

I heard enough, though, as did Tom. They had been inundated with requests since Rio and had reached a point where they needed help with it. They weren't sure what to do or what not to do. We arranged for me to meet them at their home in Heswall on the Wirral within the next few days.

I remember preparing for my meeting with Sam and wondering how to approach it. Her life would have monumentally shifted in the previous few weeks, as would have her hopes and expectations for the foreseeable future. But what most Olympians don't realise at this moment is that the path ahead will be really tough. So, I pondered what to tell her – that life would be a breeze now and that the money would roll in, or tell her the truth? ... I opted for the truth.

As soon as I entered their house, I immediately sensed the incredible bond between Tom and Sam. He cared deeply about her and she very much followed his lead through love and respect. There was an intensity about them as well. They recognised the opportunity they had in front of them. They had already met a couple of other agents, one of whom – an infamous one who will remain nameless here – immediately offered her a lingerie endorsement contract. Instantly I could tell that that had been the worst possible move with Sam. She was a really strong woman and was slightly embarrassed about the attention on the way she looked. She wanted to forge a path ahead that wasn't dominated by her looks. Sam also explained that she was contemplating retirement because she wasn't sure she could go through another Olympic cycle.

I explained to her that the hockey market or bubble wasn't big enough to make a substantial career moving forward: 'The thing is, Sam, that right now it will feel like hockey is enormously important in this country, but the honest truth is that in about three months, no one will give a shit about it.'

That was the truth, but it was a massive risk on my part. I was telling a recent Olympic gold medallist that her beloved sport would be fairly irrelevant in twelve weeks' time as people went back to watching football. I explained to her that if she wanted to make it big with commercial opportunities or future presenting work then she would need to get beyond the hockey bubble as soon as possible because it was such a limited market. To do that would mean she would have to take risks and trust me.

I am forever grateful that Sam and Tom understood what I was saying and took that leap of faith with me. After every Olympics we get a rush of medallists coming back expecting the financial rewards they truly deserve, having given everything to their sport for a number of years. A vast number of these athletes will have been earning around £25,000 or less per year and utterly dedicated to what they were doing. Rightly, when they come home with an Olympic medal, let alone a gold medal, they are desperately hoping and expecting that they will finally see the financial rewards to match their achievements. The reality is very different.

We have a surge of interest in particular athletes that do well at the Olympics but, other than the very top ones, the public quickly lose interest and – granted, this is a little bit of a generalisation – the sporting eyeballs return to Premier League Football. That is the harsh truth. This is even more emphasised if yours is a team sport because you are then competing for financial rewards with not only other successful Olympians, but also your teammates. So, I knew that if Sam and I were going to work well together, she was going to have to get her head around this as soon as possible.

If, as you read this, you don't believe me, then ask yourself this question: 'Who scored the winning goal in the Olympic final for the GB Women's Hockey team?'

I suspect very few of you knew the correct answer and, as you are reading this book, you are most likely some sort of sports fan. Most sports fans struggle to remember this name. Yet this was a huge moment in our sports history, watched by over 10 million people on BBC1. That is what happens.

By the way, the answer is Hollie Webb.

This whole process wasn't easy for Sam, though. After a month of working together, Sam had made less than £50, and this was after the Olympics! I knew we were putting in the groundwork for the rewards to come and, most importantly, for them to be sustainable, but I needed Sam to hang in there with her faith in me, which thankfully she did.

As Sam began to grab headlines, some bitching also started behind her back from a few of her GB Hockey teammates. It was really tough on her and, as strong as she is, it did affect her at times. There was clearly jealously involved, and some of them attacked her in private, but also in public. One particular teammate, whom I won't name, did an interview published in the *Daily Telegraph* that didn't mention Sam by name but made the point that some people were only getting deals because of their looks. There has only ever been one player getting significant attention other than Maddie Hinch, and that is Sam.

It was all absolute bullshit. Just petty jealousy.

Sam was getting the attention and then subsequent rewards because she went for it. She was prepared to step out of her comfort zone and seize an opportunity. She had incredible support from Tom, but she has a spirit and bravery that others just looked on with envy. She didn't make the mistake that many of her teammates made, which was to sit back and expect things to come to her. The hockey bubble is not big enough commercially. She had to generate attention beyond hockey, and she absolutely did that.

It was also not necessarily straightforward for Sam with England Hockey. They were supportive of her but there was an element of always wanting her to fall back into line to help promote the team. Sam always did her best with this, but she also needed to forge her own path, so there was this difficult dynamic where she could be held back. An athlete has one shot at this, but to keep everyone happy in these circumstances is impossible.

On a wider talking point around this matter, I think it is a common mistake many sporting governing bodies make. They are, understandably, protective about their brand reputation and their perceived commercial worth *as a team*; but the reality is that too few people support 'England Hockey' or 'British Gymnastics' or 'British Swimming' to attract major and ongoing sponsorship deals. If you're unsure on this, check how many sponsors the three organisations I have mentioned have attracted since Rio 2016. Yet those organisations have had the likes of Sam, Nile Wilson and Adam Peaty as assets, whose reach is way beyond that of the teams. To add more context to this: Sam's social media reach is larger than the entire rest of the GB Hockey squad put together; and Nile Wilson is even further ahead on this with gymnastics. The majority of fans support the individual stars, not governing bodies. Team GB have in part overcome this challenge but that is because they have all the best athletes and are literally our team representative at the biggest global sporting event. Governing bodies are not like a Manchester United, so they need to focus their attention on building up their stars and then ride on the back of that for as long as they can. Look at what UFC did with Conor McGregor – they put a huge amount of PR into him and both he and the whole organisation benefitted enormously. Rather than embracing the success of their stars, the sports governing bodies in the UK seem to be terrified that they will become bigger than the sport itself.

As Jane Allen, CEO of British Gymnastics, said to me once, 'The stars will come and go, Luke, but British Gymnastics will always be here.'

It was a telling comment.

And this is why Sam will deserve every bit of success she gets – she understood the opportunity and, in the face of criticism and jealously, then went for it. No holding back.

On the outside it might look like things fall into Sam's lap. It genuinely couldn't be further from the truth; she has grafted for every bit of success she has got. Sadly, the time has passed for many of her teammates who sat back and thought it would just come to them.

* * *

Soon after my first meeting with Sam, I rang Daisy Moore, one of the main bookers at the time for ITV's flagship show *I'm a Celebrity… Get Me Out of Here!* I knew Daisy pretty well from other clients and shows and explained to her why I thought she should consider Sam for the programme. She said she would have a think about it and eventually came back to me and said they would like to set up a meeting with Sam and me. In the context of everything I have described above, this was huge for Sam.

The Women's Olympic hockey final was watched by about 10 million people on BBC1. *I'm A Celeb* is watched by about 5 to 10 million people every night for thirty nights! The audience numbers were massive, but it was also the mainstream audience that Sam needed to break out of the hockey bubble. I didn't want to put pressure on her, but her instincts knew it was a big opportunity.

We went down to London and I picked up Sam from her hotel and tried to play down the whole thing. In fairness, I did believe that, regardless of whether Sam landed this show, she would still break through. But this show would definitely help accelerate that.

We headed up to the sixth or seventh floor of the ITV building in South Bank and huddled in a small meeting room with Daisy and her colleague, Micky, and the conversation got started. And for all the rumours about what these sorts of meetings are like, they are not interviews; they are really just a meet and greet. It was also a time for me to shut up and let it all be about Sam. That can be tough if your client goes shy, but that wasn't the case this day!

Sam was brilliant. She absolutely seized the moment and was full of personality, humour and charisma. She broke out into a Scottish accent at one point when talking about the first teacher who got her into hockey, and I could tell Daisy and Micky really liked her. I just sat there and watched her going for it.

The meeting ended and we said our goodbyes and headed for a coffee in South Bank. Sam and I were buzzing, and then I made a mistake that all agents should never make:

'You are definitely landing a spot on that show!' I said.

Never, and I mean, NEVER, tell a client they are landing a deal or job when it isn't in a written contract. Yet – boom, I went ahead and bloody did it. I just felt so sure that she had nailed it. That comment haunted me as we waited for a final decision over the coming weeks.

I contacted Daisy a few days after the meeting to get her feedback, and she said they really liked Sam and would like to look at putting her on the show. This was very exciting but there was no guarantee at this point. The process of filling a line-up for a show like *I'm A Celeb* is very much like completing a jigsaw puzzle. It is how your client fits with the overall line-up that they are looking at … and you have no idea what they are looking for, so you are completely in the dark. At this stage, all we knew was that they were keen on Sam, so we kept everything crossed.

While all this was going on, I also started to hear that Maddie Hinch had been telling people that she had already been approached about the show and was keen to do it. We knew that, in part, this couldn't be true. There is no way that they would be interested in Sam if they were already engaging with Maddie. It was a bizarre situation as Sam was constantly being asked about Maddie for the show by friends and even the press. She just had to bite her lip and keep everything quiet.

I kept checking in with Daisy, but no immediate decision was being made. It was an unbearable wait. My comment to Sam about definitely getting on the show hung over me like a shadow and there were other dynamics at play; we were turning down other shows in the hope and optimism of landing *I'm A Celeb*, but we had no guarantees. There's no question that the final decision would have had a big impact on everything Sam and I were doing, and the wait was agonising.

On 7 October 2016, five weeks after we had met Daisy and Mick, Sam and I were at the Leaders event at Stamford Bridge in London. Sam was just about to go on stage for a Q&A and my phone rang … it was Daisy:

'Break open the champagne, she's in!'

That was all Daisy needed to say. OK, I know Sam had won an Olympic gold medal eight or so weeks ago, but in our little world and in the work we were doing, this was massive! A female hockey player was going on one of the biggest mainstream shows for the best part of a month. This was a *really* big thing.

I quickly shouted to Sam to come over and told her the news. She was elated but then had to go on stage and answer questions sensibly.

The next few weeks while Sam waited to go on the show were equally difficult. She couldn't tell anyone, including her family, which was so difficult for her. We still had some very good work lined up for her during this time but *I'm A Celeb* was never far away from any of our thoughts. The bizarre thing was that the Maddie Hinch rumours continued to circulate, and we just had to continue pretending we didn't know. I wasn't quite sure who was putting them out there, but we knew they would eventually look silly.

Sam was now going to break out of the hockey and, for that matter, sport bubble without any problem, but my role very much depended on using this opportunity to line her up for work that would give her experience and profile, and, more importantly, be sustainable. As an example, Sam is a huge Liverpool FC fan and LFC TV had previously been in touch with her about doing some work with them. Sam, Tom and I chatted it through and felt this was an important stepping stone for her. Eventually it was agreed that Sam would co-host a show for them. There may at the time have been people wondering why she was doing this with such a small TV company, but she needed to gain some presenting experience, and this was the perfect place to do it. It was a friendly audience and the producers were brilliant, and very supportive of Sam. She would be able to learn and develop, and this would be the sort of work that would be a stake in the ground for her future.

We all have Sam's first-ever LFC TV show recorded. It is incredible to look back on as she has come so far since, but anyone who bemoans Sam's success is likely not to understand what she has done to grab every opportunity. She wasn't forced to do LFCTV and she's not stupid. She knew why it was important and, despite having no presenting experience, went for it. And then, significantly, she kept trying to improve. She didn't get too down when she struggled, but she grafted at it. A common mistake of many sports people is that they believe things should come to them because of what they have achieved on a sporting field, but it rarely works like that.

Sam is a brilliant example for any Olympian of how to come home and make the most of the opportunity their medal might give them.

* * *

In a previous chapter, I mentioned about how family members getting involved in someone's management can become very difficult. I have to say that in Sam's case, this is not so.

Tom, her husband, has always been a big part of everything she has done and I was initially cautious as to how that dynamic would work, but it has been brilliant for Sam and for our working relationship. Tom provides Sam with another voice that is only coming from a place of love and support, and he is another person for her to bounce things off. Generally, Tom and I see things similarly, but not always, and it has been good for Sam to have two people she can lean on. I think the reason this works is that Tom and I respect each other's roles and act as a support for each other rather than anything else. He has strong opinions, as do I, and we have both worked on how to channel that in a way that is constructive for our overall relationship. Part of that has been for me not to feel that I need total control. I respect Tom's opinion and, more importantly, how much Sam values it, so, as mentioned in my chapter about Jimmy Anderson, I have learned to advise and assist rather than be a commander-in-chief.

It is really not easy for a sporting star's other half, either during or after their sporting career. All of a sudden, their life is all about their partner and their sporting prowess; and this was exactly how it was for

Tom. Much of their lives were directed towards Sam's hockey before the Rio Olympics but post-Rio and, particularly, post-*I'm A Celeb*, everything moved to another level. The television appearance put the spotlight on Tom and all of Sam's family, and it was hard for them all. The press wanted to know everything they could about them, and nobody took the brunt of this more than Tom. Social media is brutal at the best of times, and we often forget that celebrities' partners and families feel this too. I warned Sam's family ahead of *I'm A Celeb* what it would be like, but even then, I think it shocked them. Tom is a successful businessman in his own right, but as he now jokes, he has just become a cameraman for Sam and people wanting photos of themselves with her.

Tom and Sam's partnership and our overall working relationship are unique in many ways, and I am so proud of what Sam has achieved over the last four years.

She has earned every bit of it.

Chapter 5

The Rise of Social Media

S ocial media has created the biggest dynamic shift in my job over the last five years.

In fact, social media evolves and changes things so often that it can be difficult to quantify its impact at any given moment. Further to the examples in previous chapters of how social media has affected what I do as a sports agent and, more importantly, the careers of some of my clients, a full chapter dedicated to this seems entirely appropriate.

It is not too bold a statement to say that social media now profoundly affects every single aspect of the sports industry.

I will try to give you some easily digestible examples to back this up.

In the chapter about my management of Jimmy Anderson, I explained how, back in 2011/12, we needed to raise his profile beyond the traditional cricket fan base and how we in part used his newspaper column and his sponsorship deal with Wellman to help achieve this. Put simply, higher profile meant bigger and more numerous sponsorship deals – David Beckham being your gold standard for this as every household in the United Kingdom would know who he was. However, those methods I described for Jimmy are basically dated now. Social media can circumnavigate them all. Athletes don't necessarily need that traditional billboard advertising or newspaper column inches to make the off-field money they are looking for. Online presence and content are now the powerhouse for off-field value. Indeed, every sponsorship contract I now negotiate will have social media activity very high on the list of deliverables for the athlete.

The best athlete to illustrate this with is my client Nile Wilson, whom I will talk about more in later chapters. Nile is extraordinary in so many ways and he has taught me so much about the changing landscape of commercial worth that is dominated by online presence. Nile is not in the same category as Jimmy in traditional sporting profile terms, but his off-field earnings can be as much as four times those of Jimmy's. That is simply because Nile creates unbelievable content for all his social media channels, including YouTube. He engages and inspires his audiences, and that is like gold dust to brands out there.

This sort of online activity also creates a huge 'under-the-line' fan base that some people miss. Just attend any British Gymnastics event and measure the cheer from the crowd for Max Whitlock, double Olympic gold medallist and brilliant gymnast, versus Nile. The crowd is generally full of children and teenagers – exactly the audience that Nile engages online. So, the cheer for Nile is vastly louder than for someone like Max. Children and teenagers are now far less inclined to get their heroes from billboards and BBC TV than from YouTube.

As an agent, I have to be alert to this in a number of ways. I need to help clients create worthy online presence. I can't make them into something they are not, and Nile is a genius in this space, so few will be able to do what he does; but they need some sort of standing in this space if they want to make strides commercially.

Take a look around the sports industry globally and observe which athletes, brands, broadcasters, clubs and organisations are fully aware of the point I am making, and also notice the ones that aren't. The difference is enormous, and you can spot it a mile off when you know what to look for.

A great example of this is the sports broadcaster BT Sport. They have significantly fewer sports broadcasting rights than someone like Sky Sports, so their greatest challenge is how to keep their audience engaged in between, in the build-up to and after the big sporting events that they do have the rights to. They have a lot of 'down time' in their programming. They fill this with as much as they can, but if they don't have enough rights, there is little they can do.

Their answer has been to turn to social media rather than to the playing of highlights. They have used social media to push out short-clip programming in various guises. *No Filter* has been a behind-the-scenes look at different sports, athletes and events coming up. They have also used the post-match discussions brilliantly in this manner as well. This has enabled them to keep their audience engaged on social media while they don't have that much to show on TV. Significantly, this has been supported by some of their on-screen talent with huge social media followings, e.g. Rio Ferdinand, Gary Lineker and Jake Humphrey. The effect has been excellent, and, to some degree, they have turned the concept of 'support programming' on its head.

Sports broadcasting has become increasingly competitive in recent years, with more broadcasters in the market for rights. BT Sport's example of quality support programming via social media means that a sports broadcaster can operate without having twelve hours a day of expensive sports rights. Of course, other broadcasters have followed suit but, in my opinion, they all fall behind BT Sport in quality and innovation for online content.

* * *

I want to bring Sam Quek back into this chapter about social media. As you know, our challenge immediately after the Rio Olympics was how we moved her beyond the hockey bubble because it was too small for her to build a sustainable presenting career.

Football was a clear area for Sam to work within. She had played for Tranmere as a teenager and could well have gone on to challenge as a professional footballer if she hadn't chosen hockey. She was also a lifelong and deeply passionate Liverpool FC fan. She knew her stuff – a superfan of sorts, with an Olympic gold medal hanging around her neck.

So, how would she gain some credibility within football and overcome the inevitable avalanche of 'you're just a hockey player'?

Now, don't get me wrong, this is still a massive challenge. But hands down, the best way Sam has done this is via social media, and in particular, Twitter. She tweets about football, giving strong opinion almost every day. She takes abuse but she puts her neck out there and adds humour to it all to overcome it. She is bloody brilliant with it.

Whether people consciously started to acknowledge that Sam knows what she's talking about with football is one thing, but there is no question that, subconsciously, this has happened. Her following and engagement has grown strongly and consistently over the last three years. Fans debate with her all the time and she takes it on. And bear in mind that some of the tweets back are not pleasant.

Three years after leaving the Rio Olympics as a professional hockey player, Sam had a weekly newspaper column with the *Daily Mirror*, in which she writes about football more than anything else. She also co-hosted the biggest live football phone-in show, *606*, on BBC Radio 5 live. I think that says it all.

Sam's online work has been different to Nile's, but equally as effective for her career, but to do this is not easy. In my chapter about Sam, I describe the challenges she faced from teammates, but she has also had to carry a very thick skin in trying to make an impression on social media. She had the knowledge and opinion to give her credibility within football, but to break through that takes the type of courage many don't have. Sam doesn't continually moan about trolling; she just knows why she is doing what she is doing and hangs in there.

A recent example to back this up was when Sam said in her newspaper column, as well as on Twitter and live on *606*, that FA Cup replays should be scrapped, which is actually an opinion shared in part by the likes of Gary Lineker. Sam took some fearful abuse for this and it was really tough. But she put on her tin hat and stuck it out.

Likewise, she wrote in her newspaper column that if it was not safe to restart the football season due to Covid-19, then the season should be scrapped. Again, an entirely sensible opinion but an unhelpful headline from the paper made it look like she was saying that Liverpool shouldn't be crowned champions. She didn't actually say that. Being popular with Liverpool fans, this went down like a lead balloon; and again, the abuse starts. But, as ever with Sam, there was no moaning and she just kept going.

Trolling on social media is a huge problem and a terrible reflection of where we are as a society, but if you want to achieve what Sam is, then you have to rise above it and see the big picture. If, for example, Sam took herself off Twitter in particular, then I don't think she would have accomplished some of the things she has to date. Again, it is a great example for other athletes who are retiring and hoping to forge a career in the media.

* * *

One day in my early years as a professional cricketer at Somerset CCC, I went to the bank. Having read my name, the man across the counter said to me, 'I've picked you in my Fantasy Cricket Team.'

I genuinely felt myself blush. I think I had only played one first team game at this point, so this was a big deal to me. I smiled and was a little lost for words. The man followed with: 'I only chose you because you were cheap.'

Talk about coming down with a crash! In fact, the *Daily Telegraph* used to print a 'Least Picked Players' team as part of their Fantasy Cricket League promotion. I had the honour of making that team two years on the bounce!

Colin Wells was my second team coach at Somerset CCC and my first team coach at Derbyshire CCC. Colin loved a joke and always used to say that you never wanted to make a duck on a Friday because it would be reported across the full two days of the weekend. It was better doing it during a weekday, and then you only had twenty-four hours to wait until it was 'yesterday's fish and chip paper'.

Social media has turned all of this on its head. Reporting, analysis and then criticism or praise is handed out instantly. It is impossible to stay away from it as a player. Johnny Wilkinson's famous quote, 'I don't need to read how I played in a newspaper because I will already know myself how I did', seems aged now. A player's first worry won't be the newspaper reports anymore; he or she would already have been given thousands of opinions of their performance on social media. And it is basically impossible to stay away from. To avoid it is not as simple as you coming off it. You would also need your family to stay off it, all your friends to stay off it, the local newsagent to stay off it, in fact, anyone that you might bump into to stay off it, because they will all relay to you what they have picked up on social media.

We live in a social media world of instant reaction and sound bites, with a constant challenge on sensible analysis. The Peter Moores misquote of 'data' and 'later' was a powerful example of this, as is reaction to incidents within matches or competitions.

Louis Smith has been managed by Activate for the last five years, not by me personally, but by Gab Stone. Gab managed him during the 2016 Rio Olympics. Social media had an enormous influence on his whole experience at those Olympic Games. Louis was a game changer for British Gymnastics, winning the first-ever men's gymnastics Olympic medal with a bronze in the pommel horse in 2008 at Beijing. He followed that with a silver in the London 2012 Games. At times, Louis has polarised opinion but, in my view, is much misunderstood. He's a good guy, who cares about those around him – a sensitive soul, in essence. But he is also happy to sit outside of the crowd and be an individual, and this last bit of his character can make people think he is aloof, and maybe even arrogant. It's just not the case, though.

Louis competed in the team event in which Team GB had a chance of a medal. It was a tough ask with the giants of gymnastics, e.g. Russia, China and Japan, dominating so much, but they had a chance. Louis was a specialist, meaning he only competed in one apparatus, the pommel horse. With two scores counting on each apparatus, Louis could only contribute to the team on the pommel horse. Pommel also happened to be the last apparatus to be competed for the team event.

As the competition unfolded, Team GB were in a scrap with Japan for the bronze medal. As they came to the final piece, the pommel horse, Team GB were significantly behind the Japanese. It would take extraordinary routines of the highest difficulty from Louis and Max Whitlock to give the team any chance of a bronze. Louis knew he had to go for it. The truth is that, even if Louis and Max had both nailed it, the team could have still missed out on a bronze.

Louis attempted his hardest possible routine, slipped and fell off the horse. The team's chances of a bronze were blown away. Within the next hour, social media blew up that Louis Smith had ruined the team's chances of winning a bronze medal. There was no context added that Louis had to go for bust and made a mistake when the margins of error were minute. The sound bites demanded by social media didn't allow for the substance of why this had happened to be explained, and the bloodthirsty nature of social media meant that no one was interested. Louis got lambasted.

Anyone who ever held a small gripe against Louis dived in on him and the criticism was brutally unfair. Imagine if he had played safe and scored an above average score but not enough to win bronze. Would anyone have noticed the subtlety in this? I very much doubt it.

Social media went wild and Louis felt it badly in Rio. Of course, he tried to stay away from it, but it was impossible not to feel the reaction when virtually every friend you have is on it and checks in to see if you are OK because of what they are reading. It was ten days until Louis' individual competition on the pommel horse and that was a really tough time for him. The reaction towards him was so negative that it badly affected his confidence. There were moments when he seriously considered pulling out of the individual event. Gab, who manages him better than anyone, was in Rio and talked to him all the time, as did Louis' mother. We were all concerned for him.

The social media mass didn't care about any of this. They didn't give a thought to the context around Louis' mistake, let alone consider that as a Team GB athlete, he still had another medal to compete for. In the end, Louis pulled himself together, with the support of Gab and his mum, and was ready for the individual event. Little did we know that that would then cause more drama for Louis on social media.

Louis' main competition for gold on the pommel horse was his teammate, Max Whitlock. Max was phenomenal and Louis would have to pull off a flawless and very difficult routine to beat him. As the final panned out, Louis was to do his routine second to last and Max was last. It couldn't have been scripted any better. Again, Louis knew he had to go for broke if he was to beat Max. Max's form was just so good at the time that you had to presume he would nail a very high-scoring routine.

Louis had had a brutal ten days' build-up to this moment. His confidence was badly shaken and he felt like public enemy number one. The pressure on him was immense. He started his routine but early on felt that his arm was going to slip. He could fall again. In a millisecond, everything flashed in front of him. He knew what another fall would mean, not just in failure for a medal, but in the public reaction.

In that split second, he changed his routine to something safer that he knew would most likely not be enough to challenge Max. He completed the routine and nailed his dismount. With a huge amount of relief, he sat in gold medal position but knew Max would likely follow him with a better routine, and he would fall back into silver. Bearing in mind the level that these guys are competing at and the enormous pressure Louis was under, what he did was nothing short of miraculous. Indeed, Max nailed his routine and won gold, pushing Louis into silver. It was Louis' third Olympic medal in as many games – a remarkable achievement.

As Louis climbed onto the podium to collect his silver medal, the tears flowed from him. He was enormously emotional. Very few people knew the backstory. Very few people knew about the level of support Gab and Louis' mum had given him. Very few people knew the impact that the ten days between the team and individual events had had on him. Very few people knew that he had changed his course mid-routine when he thought he was going to fall again. Very few people knew what he had been through. Most people wondered whether his tears were those of joy or sadness.

In a world without the amplification and sound bite nature of social media, Louis would never have gone through what he did. It was impossible for him to stay away from and it took every bit of energy, self-will and determination to overcome. It could have been very different.

Sadly, that wasn't the end of it for Louis and social media during that Olympic Games.

Some television camera angles caught footage of Louis' reaction when Max Whitlock won gold during their pommel horse event. There were some who interpreted that footage as showing that Louis was not gracious in defeat and, indeed, said something derogatory about Max at the time to a fellow competitor. All of it was total nonsense. Louis was disappointed not to win but deeply emotional about winning silver, as he demonstrated when he couldn't contain his emotions any longer on the podium. And he didn't say anything negative about Max. A snapshot TV angle was subsequently used to vilify Louis, and along came social media for the brutal amplification of this.

Before we knew it, the footage went viral, and the same people who were climbing into Louis after the team event came after him again. It was equally as brutal. Louis had been through so much of this in the run-up to winning silver, but now he faced it again. The tsunami of social media means there is so little you can do to stop it once it has started. There was no serious consideration of the TV footage, just irresponsible journalists feeding meat to a crowd baying for blood. That is social media, unfortunately.

Louis had just won his third Olympic medal, having been a game changer for his sport. He was part of a golden generation for British Gymnastics and instead of him being celebrated as part of that, he was attacked with social media. This wouldn't have existed before the dynamic that social media provides – sound bites, snapshots, nastiness, and never much context or analysis.

Social media is to be fully embraced and engaged with for both athletes and agents, and it has fundamentally changed our industry.

But, not all of that is in a good way.

Chapter 6

James Taylor – Career Over

I woke up in the morning to read a text from James Taylor, sent at 2.00 am, saying, 'Hey bud, I need to talk you.'

It was the start of the 2016 cricket season and James was away with Nottinghamshire CCC playing against Cambridge University as they prepared for the start of the county season. For James, it was a crucial and exciting time in his career. He was just about fully establishing himself in the England side. He had become a key member of their 50-over side and had recently returned with the Test side after a series win in South Africa. Having been overlooked so many times in his career, he was on the doorstep of everything he had worked so hard for.

This was a really unusual text to get from any client, but especially James. He enjoyed a beer but was a top professional, so late-night trouble was unlikely. He had battled with his anxiety in recent times, so that was a possibility. Maybe he had woken up and suddenly had a thought about the type of bats he wanted; that was actually most likely! But it was the fact that the message gave so little away that made me think something was coming that I would never guess.

I called him straight away.

'Bud, I am in hospital; something happened to my heart yesterday and I was in a bad way. I think it is a virus or something.'

I was trying to take stock of what he was saying but I felt in shock almost immediately. James was clearly exhausted and not well. The mention of his heart was a real worry and, as far as I was aware, not something that had ever been an issue in the past. The fact that he was lying in a hospital meant that this had to be serious.

He talked me through how he had felt very unwell during the morning warm-ups at Fenner's Cricket Ground in Cambridge the previous day and his heart had just gone wild, and he had then made the journey back to the hospital in Nottingham. It felt like he was trying to minimise it all. Indeed, the immediate chat between us was whether he would be well enough to play in the upcoming Test series versus Sri Lanka. Despite this, I could hear in his voice that he knew something very serious had happened to him. He also sounded in shock.

I arranged to see him as soon as I could get there and honestly didn't know what to expect. On a personal level, James was like my younger brother. I was worried and upset for him. On a professional level, we currently had one of England's brightest batting stars lying in a hospital bed with a suspected heart problem and this needed managing. The key consideration at the start was to make sure that inaccurate information didn't slip out into the public domain before we knew exactly what the issue was. His teammates and the media were aware that he had fallen ill, and most knew he was in hospital. Journalists started calling me for an update.

At this stage, the messaging was simple – he had fallen unwell and had some sort of suspected virus, but we were waiting for the test results to come back. The truth is that, whichever way I topped and tailed it, this was obviously worse than just having a bad case of the flu.

I remember arriving at the hospital in Nottingham and walking through the corridors to James's room, nervous about how he would be. As I walked into the room and saw him on the bed, with Jose in a chair next to him, I was shocked by how he looked. James was one of the fittest cricketers in the world. He held a decent tan from his winter in South Africa and, ordinarily, would be looking the picture of health. But he looked fucking awful. He appeared exhausted – totally and utterly wiped out. I did my best not to show how shocked I was and sat down at the end of the bed.

It was clear that whatever had happened to James was serious. He relayed what the doctors had said – something had made the rhythm of his heart go all over the place. They explained that his heart had done the equivalent of six marathons in five hours. No wonder he looked exhausted! They also told him that he was lucky to still be alive. Suddenly the gravity of the situation started to hit home. I then realised that the gaunt look on James's face was partly due to fear. He was scared. He didn't know what had happened to him.

The doctors had explained that there might be a few reasons why his heart had reacted the way it had. One of them was that a virus had affected it. However, they had also broached the subject with him that it could be a heart condition.

A heart condition.

It just sounded a bit weird, to be honest. James was so fit, and nothing had ever been a problem before. It was hard for me to get my head around it as it all sounded a bit vague but at the same time, very serious. My emotions paled into insignificance compared to the nuclear bomb that had hit James's world. He is one of the most resilient people I know and had amazing support from Jose, his mum and the rest of his family; but this was different. It felt like the shadow of this possible 'heart condition' was looming large. What was not in doubt anymore was that whatever had happened to James's heart had been severely life-threatening and he was very fortunate to have survived it.

The next few days were more of the same – Jose never leaving James's side while he had more tests and we waited for the results, while I tried to manage the information flow within the media.

I don't remember exactly when Arrhythmogenic Right Ventricular Cardiomyopathy, or ARVC, was first brought up by the doctors. It was mentioned as the possible mystery heart condition that had caused everything. It was appearing that the initial virus diagnosis wasn't correct. None of us knew what ARVC was but it was quickly being brought into context as the condition that the footballer Fabrice

Muamba had collapsed with on the field at Tottenham Hotspur Football Club in 2012 and, subsequently, brought back to life from.

I couldn't imagine what James was going through in his mind. This was now moving on to something very different than whether he would make the Test series versus Sri Lanka – this was about a young man's life that was potentially about to be turned upside down. It was made clear very early on that if they had a conclusive diagnosis of ARVC then he would be told he could never play cricket or, indeed, take on any significant exercise again in his life. In short, exercise accelerated ARVC's affects and would stop the heart. It was explained that the method to diagnose this condition wasn't straightforward, but the best was from a particular type of MRI scan that used a certain type of dye. James had the scan and we all waited.

It was now the Easter school holidays and I had taken my kids down to see my parents in Wiltshire. I remember driving down thinking about all the possible connotations for James. There was clearly something massively wrong with James's heart. If it wasn't ARVC, then what was it, and how long would it take him to recover? If it was ARVC, then everything stopped for him at 26 years old. In many ways it felt like there was going to be no easy or good outcome from this; it was just the 'never play again' element of ARVC that felt so devastating.

It was the morning of 8 April and James's mum, Carol, called me. 'He's fucked. It's ARVC. He can never play again.'

Carol is an incredible woman and she fought back the tears as she delivered this news. She was utterly heartbroken for her son. James was inconsolable and couldn't speak. He just needed to be with Jose right then and there. It was one of those moments when time stood still and there felt like nothing great to say.

There may be some people who would argue that in the big scheme of things, being told you can never play cricket or significantly exercise again isn't that bad. At least he wasn't being told he was about to die. And, of course, that is true; but this is where professional sport is unique. James wasn't just a cricketer as a profession; he was exactly that as a person. He was defined by it in his own mind and the minds of those around him. Almost everything in his life had been focused towards achieving what he aspired to on the cricket field. Almost every conversation he ever had would circle back to cricket eventually. Almost every day of his life would involve a plan or thought based on cricket.

It was in his whole being as a human.

So, being told this news wasn't just a practicality that James had to deal with. It was like taking a sledgehammer to his perceived existence on earth. At 26 years old, he had never given a thought about what was to come after cricket and was now facing a bomb as to what he was meant to do with the rest of his life. It was utterly devastating.

Carol and I found it difficult to speak. As she struggled with tears, I cried too. There was little more to say at this stage. I put the phone down and sat in the chair in my dad's office and sobbed. As I sobbed, I typed out a message to James but knew it would be a few hours before I heard anything from him. I also knew that I needed to step up for him right now. Indeed, for Jose and his whole family. They felt devastated and uncertain about what to say or do.

I spoke with Lisa Pursehouse, the Nottinghamshire CCC Chief Executive, who was James's immediate boss at his county cricket club. She was, of course, devastated, and also wonderful in that her first thoughts were for James. We needed to hear from James what he wanted to do and say, but he needed time ... as much time as he wanted, but until then, this news had to remain entirely confidential. ARVC is a complicated condition and there would need to be more consultations on this. Nonetheless, the doctors were very sure it was ARVC.

This was definitely one of the moments in my management career when I realised how personally I took on the lives and careers of some of my clients. I couldn't stop crying throughout the day and genuinely felt James's pain. I'm certainly not trying to equate his feelings with mine, but this whole thing hit me hard. I felt so badly for James. Just a moment in time and everything had changed for him.

I waited twenty-four hours and then James and I spoke on the phone. He was stoic and brave, but I could feel the devastation in every word. One of the doctors at England Cricket wanted James to wait for more consultation on his test results, but James was very clear: 'I want this announced as soon as possible. I have to retire, and I want it out there now.'

I totally understood where James was coming from. The diagnosis was almost certainly correct. He couldn't bear any more waiting. A bomb had exploded in his life and he just wanted to get on with dealing with it. More delays and secrecy would be excruciating for him. The agent in me should probably have been telling him to wait until the last possible minute to retire to retain as much earnings as possible, but I couldn't do that. He was a young man desperate for some closure so he could start the long road of healing, both physically and mentally. I agreed to start the mechanisms to get this announcement out there.

I called Lisa Pursehouse again so we could go through and agree on a press statement. As we talked, we both had to pause regularly to cry to ourselves. It was awful, but we got there eventually. Wording and timing were agreed.

I had one more conversation with the England doctor, who urged for a delay on the announcement. I understood where he was coming from, but James couldn't take any more. This was about supporting James as a human being rather than as a cricketer. If by some miracle the original diagnosis was wrong, then James was comfortable to reverse everything, but for now he needed closure.

The announcement went out four days after his diagnosis and the sporting world went crazy. The outpouring of emotion towards James was extraordinary. The cricket world was in shock, but this spread across sports fans and stars from everywhere around the globe. In some ways it was curious to watch the reaction. I guess people were struck by the finality of it for such a young sportsman. He was so young … and that was it.

Managing the media at this point was full on. Every journalist and broadcaster wanted an interview or comment from James. At this time, it was a blanket 'no', and I was heavily advising him not to rush into anything. He needed time to compose himself before he was ready to speak publicly. First and foremost, he needed to manage the next step of his recovery, which would involve going home. He would eventually need an operation to get a defibrillator fitted into his chest to restart his heart if and when it stopped due to his condition. This in itself was very tough to get his head around – his heart could suddenly stop at any time. The fragility of life was slapping him right in his face, at only 26 years of age. Prior to the operation, he had to walk around with a little bag that carried his defibrillator, which was attached under his shirt to his chest. Less than four weeks previously, this young man had been an international sports star on the world stage; now he was being helped out of hospital with a bag containing a device to start his heart if it suddenly stopped due to a heart condition. Everything had changed for him.

Once James had been settled back at home for a couple of weeks, there were three main things that I needed to manage for him. The first was relatively simple. I had to speak to his various sponsors and discuss with them all how retirement would affect their contractual arrangements with him. Bar none, they were all hugely supportive of James, so they were pretty straightforward conversations.

The second issue was a difficult one for James to cope with, but in the end, one for which we found a fairly simple solution. I realised that, suddenly, James had no structure in his life. As a professional sportsman, for all his adult life he had basically been told where to be, when to train, what to eat and what to wear. Once back home, he didn't know what to do with himself. This structure was part of his identity as a cricketer and now it was all gone. The prospect of waking up each day and wondering what to do might sound like heaven to some people, but for James it was a daily reminder that life as he knew it had fallen apart.

So I decided to set up a Google Calendar for him that we would share. I could input dates into it, and he could look at it on his phone. We obviously didn't have a lot to put into it in the early days, but we would add in his doctors' appointments, visits from his mum, visits from me … anything we could, really! It obviously wasn't anywhere near the structure of his previous cricketing life, but it was something. It gave him something tangible to base his days on. Eventually, when we started his media commitments, this diary would get fuller and fuller, and actually start to be a representation of how far forward he had progressed. It was a really simple thing but it seemed to have a very positive impact on him.

The third issue for me to manage was by far the hardest and most complicated. At some point, James was going to need to speak to the press. Everyone had made a request to speak to him and they were now politely waiting to see when he would be available. James needed to speak to them in order to gain some breathing space to get on with his recovery. The longer he didn't speak, the more people would keep asking. It wasn't the journalists' fault. This was a huge cricket story and of course they wanted to hear from James.

The challenge for me on this was twofold. Firstly, and most importantly, was James ready to do this? He was very keen to speak to the press, but I was worried about exposing him to the spotlight when he hadn't quite got his thoughts and emotions in check. Weeks or even months were not long enough to expect him to have everything perfectly settled in his mind. He also now had a heart that was vulnerable to excessive stress. Secondly, which members of the press he spoke to was very important. As a manger in this situation, you want to make sure your client covers as many broadcast outlets in as few hits as possible to gain wide enough coverage to achieve the goal – i.e. the breathing space that James sought.

Sky Sports had been a huge partner to England Cricket over the years and definitely warranted an interview, but the numbers of viewers via Sky would be a little limited, so we needed to do something with a terrestrial channel as well. The BBC would be able to provide TV, radio and huge digital coverage.

The newspapers were different. We didn't want any of them to feel they would miss out, so we decided on a round-table interview session with all of them. James would do the Sky and BBC interviews on one day, and then the newspapers the following day. All were going to be at Trent Bridge during the Nottinghamshire versus Yorkshire opening County Championship match.

I have to admit, I was extremely nervous about it all. I worried that it would all be too much for James and kept emphasising that we could pull back at any time. He was adamant that he could handle it, but I wanted to keep a close eye on everything. The Sky and BBC interviews were great – enormously powerful interviews that James actually quite enjoyed.

The next day we travelled back for the round-table with the written media. By this point in both James and my careers, we pretty much knew every cricket journalist, and most are good friends. As they entered the room, I could tell they were all very sensitive to how big a deal this was for James. Everyone sat down and I stood a few yards away from James. The questions started to flow, and James was handling it all fine. I was anxious but felt comfortable about how it was going. Then one of the journalists asked James how it felt for him to have finally reached a place in his career where he had established himself as an England regular and then it had been taken away from him. It was a fair question and nothing we hadn't expected. As James started to answer, I heard his voice wobble. He started to break down. I immediately stepped in and helped him up, and we walked into the corridor. My heart broke for him as he cried. My feelings as a big brother to him came to the fore and as I had my arm around him, he sobbed onto my shoulder. This hugely successful sportsman seemed so vulnerable. Like a child. I felt a huge responsibility towards him. He had dealt with so much in his career but the realisation that everything he had worked so hard for had been snatched away from him in this fashion was overwhelming. I urged James to stop the interviews and I would take him home, but being the stubborn bugger that he is, he said he wanted to continue. We took some moments outside for him to compose himself, and sure enough, he went back in and finished the questions. As ever, he stuck it out.

The final interview we decided to do was on mainstream TV and it would be with Piers Morgan on *Good Morning Britain*. I'm not a great fan of Piers, but I knew he would handle this sensitively as he was a huge cricket fan and had followed the story closely. This was also a different sort of audience that James would be exposed to versus his other interviews. We decided that once this was done then James would have done enough media for the time being.

James and Jose travelled down to London and stayed overnight in a hotel. I met them bright and early in the morning and we travelled together to the *GMB* studios in South Bank. Jose was to appear on the programme with James, which I was really happy about. She would be a source of comfort to him sitting next to him on the sofa, but she also deserved to be recognised for the unbelievable support she was giving him. As his girlfriend and now wife, she has always been and continues to be an amazing partner for James. As they went through to the studio I sat in the green room and watched it all on the TV screen. They played a beautiful montage of James's career and story, and then Piers conducted a lovely interview with them both. James and Jose handled it brilliantly.

I was alone in the green room and, as I watched it, again I couldn't stop crying. I felt so much for them both. They were so young and had been plunged into a situation they would never have expected to be in. They had lots of support, but the future was uncertain. My heart broke for them and I felt the weight of responsibility of managing James and all his family. They needed help.

For some of the nonsense that goes on in my line of work, this felt like real client management. I was managing a young man to rebuild his life, not whether we could stick an extra couple of noughts on a sponsorship deal. Right then and there, we didn't realise the battles and difficulties that we were to face, but I would be there for them whatever lay ahead.

We had no idea how hard the next few months would prove to be …

Chapter 7

James Taylor – Insurance

I nsurance.

You know, the thing everyone tells us is important when we are young, and we think is really boring? Well, it became pretty fucking important for James Taylor all of a sudden.

I was aware of other professional cricketers retiring due to injury and receiving some insurance compensation for having to do so, but I guess I had always seen it as being an extra to help them move on to the next thing in their life. James's situation was different and caught me entirely by surprise. I wasn't fully up to speed on what the actual insurance coverage would be if what happened to James happened to him at that age and career stage.

James wasn't retiring due to a dodgy knee that would just need careful management as he played over 50s' squash; he was retiring and wouldn't ever be able to take on excessive exercise – or stress, for that matter. What he was going to be able to do with the rest of his life was a whole new ball game. The future was entirely uncertain for him.

As has been described in James's autobiography, *Cut Short*, his total insurance payout was about £300,000. The total available was about £400,000, but cardiomyopathy was not covered in one of the policies. £300,000 is clearly a large amount of money, but for a 26-year-old facing significant ongoing medical bills and with little idea of how the rest of his life was going to shape up, this was nowhere near enough to give him security.

In truth, the lack of insurance coverage that was available to James reflected badly on everyone – the England and Wales Cricket Board, the Professional Cricketers' Association, his financial adviser and, indeed, me. There should have been better provision in place for him, and in fact for any international player in a potentially similar situation. The realisation was dawning that the insurance coverage for England cricketers was nowhere near commensurate with the modern earnings of the game, so if a player was left as incapacitated as James, there was simply not enough security for them.

Not only had James has his entire direction and meaning in life taken away overnight, he now faced real financial insecurity, which was the last thing he needed.

We challenged all we could with the insurance policies, but it simply was what it was. We couldn't rewrite the terms; it was too late, and James would only be able to get what was possible. I knew my responsibility to James was enormous but now it felt even greater. I had to help him rebuild his life and a career away from playing cricket. But this was tough. There was no warning, no preparation; we were all just thrust into this situation where I needed to find solutions for him. And quickly.

The media was an obvious area for him. He always had a strong opinion and was closer to the England team than anyone in the media at that time. But those sorts of jobs, especially the well-paid ones, don't fall off trees. And while James was high profile, he wasn't a retiring England captain, so he was going to fall into the category of having to take on a lot of freelance work and striving hard to move himself up the ladder. Nothing would be given to him on a plate. Much like his cricket career!

James's story was so interesting to the cricket world that he was in high demand for speeches and, particularly, question and answer sessions at corporate events. James didn't feel that confident taking on speeches, but he was happy to do Q&As, so alongside media work, they would form the basis of his immediate earnings. Over time, our Google calendar became full of lots of relatively small jobs. James knew he was going to have to graft away but we were all really conscious of monitoring how much he could cope with.

James, effectively, had a new body to get used to and no one was quite sure how much workload he could take on, other than we knew he had to be careful.

It was July 2016, and the start of the NatWest T20 Blast. James was asked to travel to Lord's to do some work with the ECB digital team and then do an immediate return back to Leicestershire CCC for a Q&A before their T20 match versus Nottinghamshire. He was also due to commentate on the game for *Test Match Special* that evening. This was three bookings in a day, plus a lot of travel. It was a lot for him, but I thought it would be OK. He had a car bringing him back from London, so he could relax during the drive and hopefully get some rest in between jobs.

Unfortunately, the car back to Leicester got stuck in traffic and it looked like James would be late. James got anxious about this and was already tired from an early start down to London. We were about to find out that this was not a good combination for his heart. He eventually arrived at the ground and rushed to the start of the Q&A. As he answered questions, he felt nervous, as he always did during these sessions, and then, all of a sudden, he felt like a cricket ball travelling at 100 mph had hit his chest. He was physically pushed back a few yards by this sensation.

The defibrillator had gone off ... because his heart was about to stop ...

The combination of tiredness, anxiety, and then nerves from the Q&A stressed his heart too much and, bang, it went off. To save his life. In shock, James quickly made an excuse on mic and left the room. Fortunately, Jose had driven down to Leicester that night to take him home afterwards and they immediately got in the car. It was raining so the commentary was off. James called me during the journey. He was in utter shock.

Once more, the fragility of life was smack bang in James's face. He was scared and vulnerable, all over again. He was just trying to earn a living and get back to some sort of normality, but this moment was a sharp reminder that things were far from normal. I felt terrible. I hadn't got it right this day and he had done too much. It was a sharp learning curve for me on how much he could do in one day.

The other lesson from that day was that Q&As might not be possible for him. He felt nervous in the build-up and then during them. Despite commentary being broadcast to many more people, it was the live audience that made Q&As different. We didn't rule them out going forward, but James definitely needed a few days' rest from everything. The fact was that, if Q&As were no longer possible, then we had a significant source of income ruled out for him. The insufficient insurance coverage wore heavily on James and on all of us on a regular basis.

James recovered from this shock after a few days and we decided to leave the Q&As until a couple he had booked in for the T20 Finals Day about five weeks later. I went with him on the day to make sure that, if anything happened, I would be there to support him. He was also commentating for *TMS* that day. He loved the commentary, and the *TMS* team, so that side of things was a real pleasure for him. The first Q&A, hosted by Dominic Cork, was during the break in between the semi-finals, and James was to do it alongside Chris Woakes.

Corky made an early joke about James's heart and I caught a look with James. He was pale. The sudden focus on him and his heart must have rushed his nerves and anxiety.

Oh fuck, this is happening again.

James reached for some water, but I clearly needed to get him out of there. Unfortunately, the Q&A was in full flow and James was still answering questions, although in fairly stunted fashion. I didn't know whether to step in, which would have looked bizarre to the average person watching, or leave him to stick it out. He seemed to be handling it OK, except for him looking like he'd seen a ghost.

We finally got to the end of it and I rushed over to James. As I gave him a little hug, we both knew that was the last Q&A he could do for the foreseeable future. Again, a chunk of income was simply not going to be possible.

James's media work was going well but moments like these kept highlighting how far he had to climb before life would feel some sort of normal again. And greater than that, we had something hanging over us that was far more significant …

The question everyone immediately asked after James's heart condition was diagnosed was: hadn't it ever been spotted before? It was an obvious question and triggered James and his family to look over everything they could from the past. James had been in the England Cricket system from his late teens as he made his way from age group representative teams to the England Lions squad, and then eventually to the full England squad. As a result, he had been part of their medical screenings for a long time. James's mum, Carol, remembered that there had been something in the past about a heart screening he had done. In fact, Carol remembered that they had made a trip to London for some sort of follow-up heart test because something on a screening had flagged a possible problem that needed further investigation. She then found letters that actually showed two occasions when screenings indicated that something was possibly not right and needed further tests. This was all in and around James's early twenties, and coincided with him moving counties from Leicestershire CCC to Nottinghamshire CCC and going on an England Lions tour.

James documented all of this in his autobiography, but in very simple terms, his test results got lost in an inadequate system that wasn't properly centralised at the ECB and was underprepared to deal with heart screenings. In all this time, James was making his way through the England Cricket system with a developing deadly heart condition, and little red flags were being missed by everyone.

It is not easy to describe how hard this information hit James and his family.

We were all still reeling from the difficulties the insurance coverage posed on James's future but now there was this. Everyone was hurting and recovering in their own way, no one more so than James, and this information was tough to take. James could, and probably should, have died. He had lost so much and now we were trying to process the fact that this could have been identified years ago.

I realised there was a very difficult, emotional and turbulent situation about to develop. This wasn't a case of looking for people to blame; but it was rightly a situation that we all wanted some clarity on as well as for the people involved to understand that they may have a greater responsibility to James. On one side were James and his family, and on the other side was the ECB. I was obviously on James's side, but my job was to sit in the middle and try to navigate this situation so that we didn't end up in the middle of a nuclear explosion.

Also in the middle with me was the Professional Cricketers' Association – the professional cricketers' trade union. They too should have sat on James's side but had a responsibility to try to find a way for it all to be resolved to everyone's satisfaction.

I have to say that these were some of the hardest months of my management career. I felt an enormous responsibility to James, not only in advising him as best and as honestly as I could and managing his family's emotions, but also in finding a way for him to gain some closure on the whole thing and start to rebuild his life. I felt the pressure badly.

Andrew Strauss was the Director of Cricket at the ECB at the time and an old friend of mine. Andrew is an excellent person and understood the sensitivities of the situation but clearly had to protect the ECB's position and personnel involved. I felt the PCA were a little slow in dealing with it all. Initially they wanted a quick resolution, but it felt like they were increasingly unsure as to how to resolve it all for the best.

Strauss asked for an independent report to be done on James's case and we waited for the results. They were due to arrive one week, and it was pushed back to the next, and then again. We waited and waited. Eventually, while on holiday in France, I had a call with Strauss. He informed me that the ECB were not satisfied with the thoroughness of the report and wanted it to be recommissioned, and we wouldn't be able to see the results of the first report. As I stood while on the phone watching the kids playing in the pool, I had one thought: *How the fuck am I going to be able to tell James this?*

All James had done was wait, and now I was telling him to wait some more. It was tortuous for him. We had his defibrillator going off at Leicestershire CCC during this time and so much uncertainty, and all he could do was wait. I kept pushing through all the channels I could, but it felt increasingly like I was on my own and the whole thing was just drifting. By this time, we had agreed that I would do all the meetings on my own because the stress and anxiety of it all wasn't good for James.

Ultimately, James just wanted to be listened to. He wanted people to acknowledge that mistakes had been made in a situation when he had lost his entire career and very nearly his life. As each day and week went by, frustration and anger built up. It was so difficult to manage. All I kept thinking about was if I can't find a good end to this situation, *how does James move past it?* This young man had been through so much and yet the pain was still going on for him.

Finally, I got an email from Tom Harrison, the ECB Chief Executive, asking if we could have a meeting at Lord's with James, me and James's mum. I thanked him for this but made the point that it might be best just being me if this was going to be another difficult discussion.

Tom assured me it wouldn't be. *Was this the moment we had all been waiting for?*

Carol decided not to come but James and I travelled down to Lord's on 8 November 2016, exactly seven months after his diagnosis. I felt this knot in my stomach, but I didn't want to reveal my nerves to James. He had been through so much; we had been through so much: I just didn't know how we would handle it if it turned out to be another deeply frustrating meeting.

Managing someone can be enormously rewarding, but there are times when it can be daunting. You try to shield your client from so much pressure, but that pressure has to go somewhere. I felt it on my shoulders. I desperately wanted to help James find some closure on everything that hadn't happened for him. He had so much still to do in his life, but this giant explosion still bore down on him. He just wanted to be heard and understood.

As we were shown into Tom Harrison's office, John Carr, Director of Operations at the ECB, also joined us. I could feel myself catching my breath as I waited for the conversation to start. I could also sense from James that he was guarded and waiting to see what would happen. Both Tom and John have a nice manner about them, and Tom then said it:

> 'James, before we start any of what I want to talk about, I want to tell you that we owe you an apology, and if you want me to make that public, I certainly will.'

I could feel the emotion build on me as Tom used those words. A few simple lines, but they meant so much to James and to me.

Finally, he had been heard.

I didn't want to look at James because I knew I would start crying. He had been through so much over the last six months or so and I had walked every step with him. At times, I really didn't know if we would have a happy ending. I felt this enormous weight lift off me. It was a moment I will never forget.

I have had clients do extraordinary things on sporting fields. Moments of absolute genius that brought pure euphoria to millions of people watching. Sometimes, I feel a little bit part of that, and that's incredible. But those are nothing, and I mean nothing, compared to this moment with James. This wasn't about medals, runs, victories or money; this was about a young man's life.

He had been heard.

The conversation continued around how the ECB could help James rebuild his life. It was constructive and healthy. It was perfect. I will always be indebted for the role Tom Harrison played in this. This doesn't mean someone like Andrew Strauss wasn't involved; he was, but Tom stepped up as the CEO and dealt with it sensitively. I texted Tom a little bit later to express my thanks but also to tell him that I found it quite hard to describe how much this all meant to James.

As James and I walked out of Lord's, we knew it was a turning point. It felt like he could now move forward. And do you know what? It felt like *I* could move forward. A huge weight had been lifted off me that I hadn't fully appreciated how heavy it had been. I had felt James's pain in the darkest of times, but this moment of relief and joy was something I experienced equally as well. It was brilliant.

The next few months proved even more pivotal for James, but only in positive ways. Getting his book *Cut Short* published with full approval from the ECB was a great achievement, and then for it to sell so well was equally important. Again, Tom Harrison played a great hand in this and, again, James felt like he was being heard.

And then, finally, James was asked to become Assistant National Selector to the England cricket team on a three-year contract – and they won the World Cup in his first year in the role! He had experienced so much pain and anguish, but we had reached a point where he was happy, healthy, secure and again involved in professional cricket in a way that fulfilled him.

If someone asked me to describe to them player management in one go, I would tell them about James Taylor. His story is what it is all about. Yes, there was the management of financial security for him, but most importantly, it was the management of a young sportsperson's life in and beyond their sport.

When I opened James's book and read the acknowledgements, it said:

> Luke – I don't know where I'd be without you. Thanks for being a mate and an unbelievable agent. You took a lot of the worry out of my hands and gave me a future when I thought I'd lost everything.

I read it in front of my children … and cried my eyes out.

Chapter 8

Different People Mean Different Clients

E veryone is different.

Anyone in any sort of management position will tell you this. The skill to a manager of people is being able to be sensitive and fluid to the fact that different people are motivated and triggered by different things. The great football managers are always renowned for being able to encourage their players in a variety of ways – some with an arm around the shoulder and some with a rocket up their arse.

Being a sports agent has a similar dynamic. Although all your clients are professional athletes, you could have very different characters amongst them, and you need to be wise to that. This applies to how they prepare, how and how often they like to communicate, how much they like doing off the field, and how involved they like to be in everything that's going on.

A good example would be the difference between Jimmy Anderson and Matt Prior, whom I managed at the same – both outstanding cricketers and good blokes, but very different people.

Jimmy is a very process-driven cricketer. Many will see his incredible skills with the ball and think it has all come easily to him. The reality is that it has come from hours of process-driven practice. As I have described earlier, he is a master of his craft. This side to him means that Jimmy can be exceptionally focused on what he needs to do regardless of what is going on around him. If there is pressure from the media, team dynamics or anything else, he falls back to his process and then performs excellently, nine times out of ten.

The best example I can give on this is from the infamous 2015 Ashes Test at Trent Bridge in which Jimmy took ten wickets in the

match and led England to a nail-biting and crucial win. His effort in
that match was nothing short of extraordinary. After Jimmy took five
wickets in the first innings, I received a call from Sunny Singh, who
was in charge of Slazenger Cricket, who sponsored Jimmy at the time.
Slazenger were owned by Sports Direct, owned by Mike Ashley. It
wasn't unusual for a sponsor to call during a match to chat through
something, but this was different.

> Hi Luke, I've got an interesting proposal to put to you and
> Jimmy. The boss would like to offer him a unique bonus for
> this Ashes series. If he takes five wickets in an innings five
> times during this series, he can get a bonus of £250,000. Oh,
> and he can keep this first innings haul, which means he only
> needs four more.

Ordinarily, I would never bother Jimmy in the middle of a Test match,
but this was certainly a unique offer, and a lot of money. The crucial
part to add to this is that Slazenger/Sports Direct would have wanted
to do PR around this if Jimmy had achieved it.

So, I called Jimmy and talked him through it. This was a big thing
to consider and he said he would sleep on it and call me the next
morning.

'I'm going to pass on it, mate. If I manage to achieve that and then
it is heavily advertised, then I don't want it to look like I was just
chasing money. It's about winning the Ashes.'

It was another example of why Jimmy is truly an England cricket
legend. So, the offer was declined, and Jimmy got on with the match.
Others may have been distracted by this but not Jimmy. He actually
got five wickets again in the second innings, so that bonus could
have seemed even more gettable. His decision to decline the offer
could have nagged away at him. But it didn't bother Jimmy. He never
brought the bonus up again and just let it go and went back to his
process of doing what he does on the cricket field. More emotional or

fragile cricketers could have let this linger in their head throughout the whole series. In the end, Jimmy didn't achieve five five-wicket hauls in the series, but England won the Ashes and he was a massive part of that.

In essence, Jimmy just wanted to get on and deliver his skill as best he could. As a quiet and insular person, he was happy for me to handle things away from the field and keep him briefed as much as was necessary. I had to find a flow with Jimmy whereby I understood what he was about and fit within that.

Matt Prior was basically the cricketer I wanted to be! Brilliant and dynamic with bat and gloves, and an exceptional character for the England team through his time with them. Matt was very much more of an emotion and feel-based person than Jimmy. This meant that when he was feeling good, he was often red hot, but on the flip side, he could be affected badly in the opposite way. Matt was sensitive to the environment around him, whether that be team dynamics, the media or stuff off the field. As an example, during the time of the KP fallout, few were attacked as much as Matt and that was really tough on him. As a manager, I had to try to support him as best as I could with that. I actually don't think I always got it right with Matt.

Matt was also full of energy and always interested in what else was going on in the world. He would want to be involved with discussions with possible sponsors and be kept updated on everything. It is why it doesn't surprise me that Matt has made a success of running a professional cycling team and now nutrition brand. He always had much more to him than cricket. This meant that while I managed him it was a very different dynamic to the one I had with Jimmy. Matt would love regular updates whereas Jimmy was fine to be informed when things had progressed to a certain level.

Neither way was right or wrong, but as a manager I needed to be sensitive to the difference in the two of them.

This point I am making is not just about being aware of the differences in your clients but also in how you operate. I have definitely been guilty in the past of just trying to make clients fit into the way I wanted to operate rather than meeting them in the middle. Communication is a classic example of this. I am happy with information being passed on to me via emails and don't mind if it is a lot at once, but for some clients, they didn't want that. They rarely checked their emails and found it hard to process information in that way, and would much prefer a thirty-minute coffee break to talk it through. So, for me, it was much more convenient to do an update on email, yet if I just forced that on a client who didn't respond well to it then I was just creating a problem further down the line.

There are also some clients who want lots of contact; multiple times a day wouldn't be unusual, but for others, much less so. Somebody like Simon Mignolet is very intelligent and self-sufficient, and definitely didn't need to chat to me every day.

Also, the type of communication would vary. Some would want to discuss their performance with me, and others would definitely keep that separate for their teammates and coaches. It would all vary from person to person and the best agents are the ones who can adapt well to each individual.

And as in life, there are some personalities you blend with better than others – and this isn't specifically yours or the client's fault. It is a bit like a marriage that doesn't work. Sometimes there just isn't that essential chemistry, trust and flow between you that is needed at that particular time. And I stress, 'at that particular time'. For one reason or another, one or both of you are just not in a place at that time that makes the relationship work. However, I have to say that I have gained this perspective having done this for a long while; it certainly doesn't feel like that at the time when things go south. It can feel personal, but it really isn't.

In 2012, I identified the cricketer Nick Compton as someone I would like to sign. He had yet to be picked for England, but I was sure he would be fairly soon. It wasn't just the weight of the runs he scored but it was also the manner in which he scored them. He batted like a

Test match player. He was also a handsome guy and I thought he could have a career in the media after his playing career finished. I managed to make contact with him and went down to Somerset, where he was playing, to meet him for coffee. I had played against Nick during my career but had never had a proper conversation with him.

My first impression was that I really liked Nick. He was different. He was introverted and a bit complicated; but there was a steel to him. He gave off an uberconfident manner, but I sensed a vulnerability within him that needed some support. I explained what I saw in him and my style of management, and we seemed to connect. The meeting went well, and he decided he wanted to work with me. I was genuinely delighted.

Nick continued to score a lot of runs for Somerset and I started to generate some more focus on him in the media. Momentum was definitely gathering for him to be called up to the England squad. All seemed to be moving in the right direction. However, as this started to happen, things were becoming a bit difficult between us, and I genuinely had no idea why.

Over the next few weeks it all became really awkward and strained. He did get selected on the winter tour for India but by then things had fallen apart between us. I never really understood why and took it very personally.

Moving forward seven years to last year and I received an email from Nick. He apologised for his actions at that time and acknowledged that he had other people in his ear, and that was confusing his thinking. He didn't need to send that email and it said an awful lot about him that he took the trouble to do so. He had been through a lot in those seven intervening years, so I massively appreciated him reaching out like that. We have met up since and have a good relationship again.

This was just an example showing that, at that time, Nick and I didn't blend. Although it sounds personal, it really isn't. Nick was just about to play for England; years and years of dedication and hard work was all about to pay off as his dreams were to be realised. This is an extraordinarily unique moment in someone's career and life. If he had other people in his ear, which can happen at these times, then it is a tough situation to manage. It just wasn't our time.

I also managed the highly talented young cricketer Haseeb Hameed, for a little over a year, and this was another working relationship that didn't work out at the time. As much as I tried, it just didn't seem to flow in the right way.

I watched Haseeb a lot during his breakthrough season for Lancashire CCC and then when he made his England debut in India. There was no doubt in my mind that he had the ability to be a 100 Tests cricketer. He had the necessary talent, temperament, desire and dedication in abundance and although his game appeared to suit the longer format, I actually believed he had it within him to develop a shorter format game as well. I thought he was the real deal.

After chasing him for a few months, he eventually signed with me and I was delighted. He was a really nice young man and I seemed to get off to a good start with him. I got on well with his family, who clearly had an enormous influence on him, especially his brothers and father. However, our start did coincide with him recovering from the bad finger break he suffered while on tour with England. He needed surgery and the finger was a bit of a mess post-operation. It meant that that winter was a little disrupted for him in practice and preparation.

I have seen players practise a lot, I was one of them, but no one compares to how much Haseeb would with his father! They would be practising in the indoor centre at Old Trafford whenever they could. Indeed, later in that year they asked me to source them an indoor centre to train in over Christmas Eve, Christmas Day and Boxing Day! They were relentless, and Haseeb's father was an enormous driving force behind that.

Ultimately, Haseeb's form began to deteriorate badly during that next season. He seemed to be trying to play in a slightly different style to what we had seen of him before – much more aggressive. It can often happen to a young batsman that after playing for England, they feel a pressure to play like a dominant international player and get away from what made them good in the first place.

He was also adamant that he should be playing a full role in Lancashire CCC's shorter format teams in the 50-over and T20 competitions. I have to admit, I didn't think he was quite as ready as he and his family thought for the shorter formats. Lancashire were not convinced either and although they played him in the 50-over competition, it felt like they were trying to accommodate him. Tensions were steadily rising between Haseeb, his family and the club, and I was in the middle, not necessarily finding a solution to it all. It certainly wasn't for the lack of trying, but our relationship was just not flowing throughout this time.

As Haseeb's form and relationship with Lancashire CCC were sliding badly, he asked to meet me for a coffee and told me he wanted to find a new agent. I genuinely thought the meeting was going to be about what Haseeb wanted to do with his career next. We still had considerable time left on our contract for one thing, but he was also at a crisis point with his form and something needed to change on that front. I thought he was going to discuss with me a change in his coaching or that he wanted to move clubs. But this is the decision he wanted to make.

There's no doubt that a part of me felt annoyed when he told me. But like I said at the start of the book, as an agent, you are often the first to be blamed when things are not going well, regardless of whether that is fair. However, I clearly wasn't managing to help him get through this general rut he had got himself into. Our character dynamics were just not mixing that well. It feels personal, but it really isn't.

As with the Nick Compton situation, finding a good working relationship with a client can be very much about timing: where you are at versus where they are at and what they need. Does it blend and work well? It isn't necessarily as personal as some people think or feel. At certain points in time it can work, and at others, unfortunately not.

Chapter 9

How You Sign Clients

There always seems to be a fascination, when people ask me about my job, around how an agent actually signs a sports star. I think it is another thing that Jerry Maguire is responsible for! What did he call himself – 'King of the house calls. The Master of the living room'?

But I do understand the fascination. I remember hearing a story while I was still playing cricket that the agent who finally signed Sachin Tendulkar wrote him a cheque for $5 million as a signing-on fee to show him how confident he was in making all that money back and more. I don't know how true that is, but it definitely caught my imagination at the time. I think the fascination centres on the thought that you could sit opposite one of the biggest stars in sport, an icon, and convince them to put a big part of their career in your hands. To be able to win that sort of trust seems irresistible to the imagination of someone outside of the sports management bubble.

So, in this chapter I want to talk you through the process of signing a client, but I also want to talk about how you lose clients, because the two processes go hand in hand. When you lose a client, it almost always means that someone else has succeeded in signing them!

With some young sportspeople, there can be an equal fascination with having an agent. It can feel like a thing of status to them. Phrases like 'Yeah, I just need to check that with my agent' and 'I'm meeting up with my agent to chat through some potential deals' appeals to their egos in the dressing room. This is more the case in team sports where the swirl of changing-room chit-chat is a powerful and dangerous mechanism. Indeed, dealing with changing-room rumours is a bit of a nightmare for us agents. I always tell my young clients the same things:

> Don't believe what you hear in the changing rooms.
> Take 20 per cent off any number you hear someone say.
> Keep your business to yourself!

The ego-driven desire to have the status of an agent is not a healthy one for young sportspeople. It makes them look for things that are simply not there. It also makes them likely to sign with anyone. There was a well-known cricket agency that a few years ago simply bombarded young cricketers with messages on Facebook in a quest to make contact and then sign them. It was just a numbers game – sign up as many as possible, hoping that one or two will become future stars. Unfortunately, players desperately looking for an agent were susceptible to this sort of approach. This has never been my style because I think it is morally wrong and also because I think you are just lining up future problems for yourself as an agent. You might sign up a load of players, some of whom are fairly mediocre, and two things will happen: 1. You can't manage that number of people so some get very unhappy with you and damage your reputation; 2. You spend too much time on players who are not commercially viable and that takes away from the time and energy you need to be putting into the players who will be very successful.

This dangerous dynamic morphs itself in a different way with football. Young footballers are less likely to be signed via social media, but it can definitely happen in nightclubs. It has been known that the biggest football agent in the UK in a particular year had previously been ... a VIP host at a London nightclub. Young players were coming into the club, he was looking after them, their friendship and trust grew, and the next thing you know is he has become their agent. I'm not commenting on the job that particular guy did for his players, but the manner in which they decided to hand over their careers to him had to be a worry.

Thankfully, this sort of issue doesn't occur amongst currently established sports stars or ones on the way up who have already been highlighted as a future star. They are much more careful about who they work with. So, to quickly dispel that myth – you are not going to become Cristiano Ronaldo's agent by sending him a message on Facebook!

To sign one of the people I reference above is generally a much longer process, but it always starts with a contact. Someone or something that links you together. It can be a mutual friend or business contact, or a sponsor that is shared between one of your existing clients and the new potential client. The reason this contact needs to be there is that this calibre of potential client is very cautious about who they let into their world. You have to remember that they have likely been the star in their family and even in their community all their lives. So, they will have had people hanging on to them and asking things of them all the time. They will also be extremely wary of the media and falling into any traps, so it is simply not possible to just walk into their lives.

Clearly, one client can recommend you to another, and that has happened to me. Jimmy Anderson was amazing for me in helping me sign Haseeb Hameed and Matt Prior. But actually, this dynamic can backfire on you a little. Top clients want to feel they have your full attention. They might love you and recommend you to someone else but then feel slightly put out that you have someone else around who takes your attention away from them. It feels like you're threading a needle at times, trying to grow what you do and keep everyone happy. It might actually be a dynamic that is impossible to always get perfectly right.

You start with a mutual contact who then makes an introduction or passes over contact details, and the whole thing starts to feel a bit like a blind date! I have to add that I have always felt a massive advantage having been a professional sportsman myself. For one reason or another, it often affords me a lot more initial trust than I suspect others who haven't played sport at that level may get. And I think this is the case because the potential client feels that I likely understand what their life is like – the pressure they are under and what is required to achieve what they want to. Trying to connect with someone who doesn't understand this would be much more difficult for them, so I have definitely benefitted from this in the past.

Sportspeople are often brilliant at their sport but beyond useless at organising themselves, hence the need for agents. That means, trying to meet up with a potential client is never straightforward. It takes some perseverance to get a date in the diary and usually requires you moving heaven and earth to make it as convenient for them as possible. More often than not, they will want to bring someone with them whom they trust – a family member, lawyer or accountant. I actually welcome this. If you have belief in your abilities as an agent, then having more people there to ask questions of you can only enhance your case. You also want the client to feel absolutely secure in whatever decision they make, so it helps having other people there who will assist them with that decision.

The location for the meetings can be anywhere really, but hotels are generally a favourite. They are always seen as relatively neutral and it means you don't have too many prying eyes to worry about. The bigger London agencies will likely try to invite prospective clients into their swanky offices, but that is rarely possible for a sportsperson balancing training and everything else that goes with their schedule in between performing.

In my opinion, the absolute key to these meetings is preparation. By the time you arrive you need to know everything you can about the potential client – and their family, for that matter. OK, this sounds a little stalker-like, but it really isn't. It is just vital for you to understand them as best as you can before you meet them – their upbringing, their challenges, their best moments, their worst moments, their current sponsors, their previous sponsors, their beliefs, what makes them tick, whether they have a partner, how much you estimate they earn, identifying if and what problems they have had in the past with agents … the list goes on and on. This preparation also includes figuring out how you would work with them. How would you help them beyond the point they are at? You need to have a really clear view of this in your mind. This includes where you think they have made mistakes in the past or, more politely put, where you think they could have 'better maximised their opportunities'!

These meetings need to be precise and focused; as soon as they meander, you are losing. The reason for this is you are not facing a business person who is used to being in long meetings; you are dealing with a sportsperson who doesn't need the whole thing to get over-complicated. They need to gain a very fast understanding as to how you will benefit them. Elite athletes have to focus so heavily on their sport that anything that could seem too difficult or complicated, including an agent, will put them off enormously.

This is why I never think doing a presentation in these meetings works well. It can become clunky, business-like, and you risk losing their concentration. I don't take notes in with me; I memorise all the information I need. Again, this is all in the preparation. By having everything in your head, it means that when questions are fired at you, you are able to answer them as naturally as possible.

Over the years, I have steered clear from telling them what they might want to hear. I just tell them exactly what I think and exactly how I work. If that doesn't fit for them then I would rather we were all honest about it at the start. This goes back to my point about not setting yourself up for future problems. For example, I travel a lot, so if I tell a new client that I will be having coffee with them every Tuesday and Thursday, then I am lying and can expect a problem when they flag it up with me that we are not doing this. The start of the relationship needs to be on an honest footing; otherwise it can all blow up in your face. Generally, for you to be sitting in this meeting means one of two things: either they have had a problem with a previous agent, or they have never had an agent and your meeting is one of a few they are having. This means they are looking for a clear solution. If you are not precise enough, then you have little chance.

However, I do believe that if you are getting to the point of a face-to-face meeting then you have a reasonably good chance of success. I would estimate my success rate from these sorts of meetings as 75 per cent, and even the 25 per cent that don't lead to anything immediately can do so later down the line. As I have said throughout this book, successful relationships in sports management are often built on the right timing for both parties. Sometimes potential clients decide to stick with what they have or go with another agent, but you could still have made a good impression, and they may come back to you later.

One of my favourite and equally funny meetings to sign someone was definitely with Haseeb Hameed. He asked me to come to his family home in Bolton one night, which I happily did. As I arrived at the house, I was warmly welcomed by Haseeb and then his father. We quickly moved into the lounge and I sat down at the end of one of the sofas. As we exchanged pleasantries, Haseeb's mother came in to say hello and then both his brothers and his sister arrived. They were all so friendly … and then they too sat down. I suddenly realised I was going to be presenting to the whole family, not just Haseeb and his father! Indeed, his sister explained that she would be taking notes throughout the meeting. Next, a small table was placed in front of me, which puzzled me to begin with. I presumed they thought it would possibly help me if I needed to take notes. But then Haseeb's mother started bringing in food. Ah, OK, we were all going to eat while we spoke … but no, the food was just for me! Don't get me wrong, Haseeb and his family were showing me beautiful hospitality, but I now realised I was going to have to present to the whole family while eating at the same time. With each mouthful I took, I felt like they were all watching me, and the chances of some food awkwardly falling out my mouth were very high!

I was used to potential clients bringing another person with them but never the entire family, and then for me to have to eat at the same time was a different sort of challenge. One of Haseeb's brothers came over as a really strong character during the meeting and it gave me an early signal that his family were going to be a significant factor in how everything played out with him. This may have been unusually strong, but it would also be equally unusual for the family to have zero involvement. There is a balance to it all.

I thought the food thing was just a one-off with Haseeb, but it actually happened every time I visited the house in the evening. It was very sweet of his family, but I did have to remind myself not to eat each time before I went.

I mentioned at the start of this chapter that while talking about signing new clients, I also have to talk about losing clients. The reason for this is that the two processes go hand in hand. When you are signing someone, it more often than not means someone else is losing them, and vice versa. Like monkeys climbing through tree branches, clients rarely let go of one branch before grabbing onto another. So, when I begin to experience difficulties with a client, I know that I'm probably not getting everything right, but equally likely is that there is another agent in their ear.

Your clients being poached by other agents is a reality that potentially exists within the industry 24/7. There are clearly some agents and agencies that are more likely to do it than others. Jimmy Anderson left Activate to join M&C Saatchi Merlin, and that was the second time we had lost a client to them. The first was Ashley Roberts. M&C Saatchi Merlin is a successful and, importantly, big London agency led by Richard Thompson, a talent manager who has been well known over the last twenty years. However, to be crystal clear, I definitely wouldn't say they were poached. Indeed, my opinion is that you have to recognise the reality of the industry – if you manage excellent clients who thrive with you then, of course, other agencies will have their eyes on them and are likely making informal approaches all the time. An informal approach can simply be meeting one of your clients at an event, and this is likely to happen. If there are weaknesses that have opened up with your client, then something could come of this. We work in an industry where people will try to undercut you all the time so the strength of your relationship with your client needs to go beyond any contract between you, otherwise there could be trouble.

Having said all this, there are some agents who will actively make sure they don't do anything unethical in approaching potential clients. I have worked alongside Neil Fairbrother in the cricket industry for many years and he is definitely one of those people. He is an excellent agent and a good friend. Because we work in such a close space and we tend to work with the same calibre of player, there have always been occasions when we are trying to sign the same player or there has been the potential for one of our players to look to join the other. But we have never had a single issue with each other.

I have tried unsuccessfully to sign Jonny Bairstow a couple of times and the first time was when he was thinking of leaving International Sports Management, the agency that Neil Fairbrother worked for at the time. When I spoke to Jonny about things, I did stress that he needed to have everything fairly squared off with Neil before I could talk to him about it in more depth. I have absolutely no doubt that Neil would do exactly the same if it was the other way round.

There are also times when you have to go head-to-head with another agent you know well, and I also believe the same level of respect needs to be afforded. I was trying to sign the England Women's captain, Heather Knight, a couple of years ago, and at the same time, she was approached by Neil and his agency. When I met with Heather to convince her to sign with me, I tried to be as honest as I could about what a good agent Neil was. There was no point saying something that wasn't true. She would meet him eventually and make her own mind up. The industry is ruthless enough without getting caught up in the nonsense of some agents' behaviour. Ultimately, if you are good at your job then good clients will come to you.

Sports management is a world of signing people and trying not to lose people; and while you are trying to sign people, others are trying to sign your clients. So, it is a never-ending cycle. But, as tough as it is at times, it is not something to take too personally.

Chapter 10

Nile Wilson – The Exceptional

I first met Nile Wilson and his dad, Neil, in Starbucks at Leeds railway station in March 2017. The glamour of sports management, hey!

It was actually a meeting I went into being entirely unsure what would come from it. Nile was already being managed under my company umbrella but by a different manager, Gab Stone. Gab, a brilliant guy and manager, had to step away from the role for a period of time so our meeting was to decide what would happen with Nile's management going forward.

I wanted him to come on board with me. I had watched from a distance and was really impressed with what he and Gab had done so far. Nile was definitely different – an enormously gifted gymnast but with the charisma and personality to take him beyond his sport. As they say, 'there was something about him'.

However, I knew that as much as I wanted Nile to stay under my management, he and his dad might decide to look elsewhere. Gab was their guy and athletes rarely sign for companies; it is normally a person that they connect to. So, there was a strong chance they might walk away.

I was really impressed with Nile from the start of the meeting. He was ambitious, broad-thinking and certainly not your average professional sportsperson.

He talked about 'changing the game', which for a 21-year-old at the time was a pretty big thing to say. He used the phrase to describe his burning aim to change what anyone thought was possible in gymnastics; and this wasn't just in performance and medals, it was with regards to any area within the sport. He believed he had the ability to grow gymnastics beyond traditional thinking.

Nile was a potential Olympic gold medallist at the time and in 99 per cent of cases, that would be more than enough to persuade someone they wanted to manage him. But I was always looking for people I believed could transcend their sport, and this was because I knew that someone's spotlight in any sport was limited. And, that every sport paled into relative insignificance compared to football. So, if someone wanted to make it 'big' and I wanted to help them and be part of that journey, then I needed a client who had that ability.

Nile was this. And more.

It might sound a bit dramatic but, in my opinion, Nile was and is a visionary within his sport.

I wanted to manage him, and I knew we were a good fit. But I didn't know if he felt that same connection. A bit like a first date, really!

The meeting went well, though, and we all decided to give it a few months' trial … and the rest is history. Since then, our partnership has been exactly what I thought it could be, but – and this is really important to say – for all my experience in the sports industry, Nile has rewritten almost every rule I believed in for sports management. As much as I might have helped him, he has entirely opened my eyes to the new era of sports management and how the industry has evolved and grown.

At the start of 2017, Nile had approximately 10,000 subscribers on YouTube; by Christmas of that year, he was approaching 750,000 subscribers. The growth was enormous and everything in Nile's world changed with it. Before I get into what that change looked like for Nile, it is important for me to address how he achieved this and what my role in it was.

The first thing people should realise is that Nile had been vlogging since he was 15 years old. Fellow gymnasts, coaches, family and friends all thought he was daft for doing it, but in true Nile style, he knew what he wanted to do and stuck to his guns. He had picked up the bug for creating content at an early age. So, by the time he became one of the fastest growing YouTubers in the country, he had been mastering the art for a number of years already. This point is so relevant for elite sport in general. As fans or viewers, we often see a moment of brilliant achievement and put it down to being a natural born ability, but the truth is that it is the result of years and years of practice and harnessing of that natural talent. For Nile, YouTube was no different.

I have as many professional athletes approach me about 'doing what Nile has done on YouTube' as I do ones who give up when they realise how hard work it is. It takes long hours of thought, filming and editing. It most definitely isn't easy. Also, and crucially, Nile's content creation came from an authentic place. He wanted to show everyone why gymnastics is the greatest sport in the world. This was something he believed in passionately, not something he was forcing. There is obviously a style and technique to being good on YouTube, which Nile grasped quickly, but the place he was coming from to create things people would enjoy watching was very real. It is another common mistake I see people make on the platform when they are forcing content out there that they think will be successful, rather than it being something they are passionate about.

So, Nile has a natural feel for what will make good content but was grooving that over the years to become faster moving, better planned and more polished. His first video that went viral on YouTube, 'Ultimate Gymnastics Challenge', which has now had over 10 million views, was the catalyst for this growth but was also a creation resulting from many years of hard work. That video catapulted Nile's channel to significant growth but the key then was how he capitalised on it. He seized the moment and realised that his Ultimate Gymnastics Challenge videos had the ability to go viral, so Episode 2, 3 and so on followed. But, at that point, Nile didn't know why they were going viral. So, to some extent, I guess this is where I came into play.

YouTube is a beautiful mix of content creation and data. The data is available to anyone on YouTube, but few look at it closely or even wisely. Indeed, the more successful you become on YouTube, the more data Google make available for you to study. You can find out useful TopLine information about who is watching but, importantly, you can also find out why certain videos go viral, i.e. where the traffic comes from. YouTube's algorithms place videos on your page that it believes you will like as 'Suggested Videos'. When a video goes viral, this is very much working in your favour as the algorithms are pushing your video to many more people outside of your subscriber base. As an example, we discovered through looking at the data that one of Nile's Ultimate Gymnastics Challenge videos that was going viral was getting significant traffic from a video someone else had created of a bodybuilder trying gymnastics, which was also going viral. YouTube's algorithms were pairing these two videos together and helping us with grabbing views. It showed us that if your video was able to tap into two different audience bases then you had a much better chance of it being viewed beyond your current base. This wasn't rocket science, but something we wouldn't have known if we hadn't looked at the data. Nile then started creating videos where he tried other sports, sometimes with other high-profile people and sometimes without. Almost always, these videos worked very well.

There have also been times when we wanted to adjust the balance of Nile's male versus female viewers. Gymnastics has a huge female grassroots following but Nile's audience at one point was male skewed. Once we looked back at it, we realised that almost all his videos featured boys or men and there wasn't that much for girls. So, Nile started to collaborate with girls and women and therefore create content that might appeal more to females. Like clockwork, Nile's female audience started to grow significantly.

As a manager, you have to constantly park your ego and quickly understand what you are good at and what you are not good at. It is important to seek help and allow others to lead in your areas of weakness. I don't have even one per cent of the creative feel that Nile has so I don't get involved with that other than when he asks my opinion. I realised my role was around the data. Perhaps that is boring, but important, nonetheless. My job was to look at it and relay to Nile what could be his next sensible move.

The truth is that it worked bloody well, and Nile now has a platform with more than 1.4 million subscribers, has had over 225 million views and was listed at number thirty-seven in the UK's biggest online influencers in *The Times* in 2019.

This online growth changed so much in Nile's world. His profile, albeit online, skyrocketed, and the levels of engagement he was getting via his YouTube channel and Instagram were higher than any other UK sportsperson on those platforms. To give you an example, we generally look for engagement levels on social media of around 5 per cent to 7 per cent to be considered very good, and Nile was consistently hitting 15 per cent.

This change for Nile was predominantly positive but not always, and the negative side definitely needs discussion. But let's start with everything positive.

Nile was able to launch businesses that fed us his online presence, specifically, a website called Body Bible, selling gymnastics-based training programmes and his own line in merchandise. Both became enormously successful overnight. But, most importantly, his ability to attract brand partnerships went up exponentially. In the first half of 2017 we would discuss appearances that might earn him £500; by the second half of the year, these discussions centred on thousands of pounds, and then shortly after, tens of thousands of pounds. This was all while he was earning about £26,000 a year as a professional gymnast.

To give you an example, we launched a new version of his merchandise during 2018 and we sold over £20,000 worth of products in the first twenty minutes. It was completely bonkers.

Nile wasn't on many city centre billboards or TV adverts that some of the other more 'mainstream' sports stars were on, but he was making much more money than most of them. It opened my eyes entirely. Not just in the numbers involved but also in the capability he now had to engage a fan base with brand or business activity. He was like a walking/talking production team, and we could offer brands so much more.

The moment of stark realisation for all of this came when, towards the end of 2017, Nile shot an online advert for Coca-Cola that took one day and earned half of his entire earnings from gymnastics that calendar year. Nile was yet to be at the peak of his gymnastics career from a performance point of view but from an out-of-the-gym-earnings point of view, things were flying. We had a nice team working around him, including his sister, Joanna, and all was going really smoothly.

As I said before, almost all of this was positive for Nile. He was absolutely doing things in gymnastics that others were yet to achieve, but it also altered the sense of reality for his world.

YouTube, in particular, was a bit like having a camera crew following you around every day. Everything people saw of Nile on screen was him, even if he was a bit more animated than normal. However, suddenly it was all being judged by views. He was continually 'on show' and always being judged by a number. This slowly shifted his reality, which in the coming months and years would have a profound effect on him.

Professional sportspeople are judged constantly and get pretty used to it. But this is almost always within the context of their sporting performances. Suddenly, Nile was receiving a new level of attention, with not only his performances in the gym being judged on camera, but also his performances in life. At the time, none of us realised how wearing this would be for him.

To add to this, his family and friends became online stars because of the exposure they all received from Nile's channel. His dad, Neil, was nicknamed 'The YouTube Sensation' and the whole family were on show. Attending gymnastics events to watch Nile now became a difficulty for all of them. Queues for photos with Neil became longer than with most of the gymnasts themselves! All of this was brilliant fun, but under the surface it was taking its toll on Nile. He was starting to shoulder more and more pressure of being constantly on display and everyone near him now being part of the show.

I believe Nile started to develop a love/hate relationship with it all. There was a part of him that loved the attention and all that it brought to his life, but there was also a part that needed a break from it once in a while. It was a bit like a comedian always being asked to say something funny. It was exhausting and there was no break from it because there was this expectation that he needed to post a vlog at least once a week. And where did that expectation come from? I guess from all of us. We just got used to it and were loving the journey – the fun, the progress and, of course, the money. But Nile was so new to me in many ways. He was, and still is, so different to anyone else I have ever managed, and I wish I had realised more quickly what this might do to him. It was chipping away at him without any of us seeing it.

Being on show all the time is brilliant when things are going well, but when life hits some bumps then it can be really tough. Nile was the guy with all the answers. He was the person we all wanted to be – positive thinking, likeable, fun and with a clear vision of where he wanted to go in life. But when suddenly Nile didn't feel like this, he still felt the pressure of being that guy because that is what the show 'demanded'. He had this whole persona that he needed to live up to.

When Nile started to experience some real difficulties with his mental health, his mind wandered to how he could go on camera and say he didn't have the answer to everything. It wasn't about showing weakness; he was fine with that. It was about not wanting to let anyone down. He felt a responsibility to everyone watching and fed off their affirmation via likes and views.

There were times when it felt like he was just fed up with YouTube and had hit a creative block, but there were also the times when he felt there was something darker underneath it all. He resented the trap that he found himself in. Then, when he produced content that didn't hit the expected numbers, it chipped away at him even more.

'I'm not that guy they think I am.'
'I'm not that guy they want me to be.'

Young professional sports stars cope with more attention and outside influence than ever before because of social media. They can't escape it. The whole of their generation is on social media; it is what they know. Asking them to ignore it is going against their entire upbringing. So, social media is in their lives, love or hate it. It makes the environment young sports stars live in more challenging than ever. The level of affirmation that young people, not just sports stars, now get from social media is very worrying, in my opinion. An alternative reality has been created, and for Nile, it was like this but on steroids.

I only started to see it all for what it was when the signs of his deteriorating mental health were impossible to ignore. And the crazy thing is that I have had my own well-documented battles with mental health issues – I knew this area! Helping Nile in this situation actually taught me so much more about mental health, particularly in a sportsperson like Nile. He is utterly inspiring to be around, and I speak to him multiple times a week, but the deterioration for him was very gradual and difficult to understand alongside other changes that may have been going on in his life.

For example, Nile was starting to go out on the town with his friends more than normal, but he was 23 years old and had always enjoyed a night out. It just seemed to be happening a bit more than previously. He was having difficulties with creating new content, but wouldn't we all feel fatigue around this having done it relentlessly for so many years? He was shell-shocked when he lost a huge amount of advertising revenue from his YouTube channel due to music copyright issues, but, again, wouldn't that hit us all hard if we had put that amount of work into it? He was becoming more distant from his family, but maybe that was just a natural progression as he moved out of the family home and started to live his own life. He was finding it very difficult to deal with the injuries he was getting, but that would be the same for any athlete.

All of these could just be relatively normal things in his life, but for Nile, they were part of a slowly deteriorating pattern of behaviour and mental health.

He wasn't able to see it at the time, but his success had created this trap. Mentally, he was deteriorating, but he felt an increasing pressure to be 'Nile', both in and out of the gym. His sense of reality was fading and was being replaced by coping mechanisms. Unfortunately, those coping mechanisms were becoming self-destructive patterns of behaviour. His mental health was leading to some of this behaviour, and then his behaviour was making his mental health worse – a spiralling situation that he couldn't escape from.

Eventually it hit a big enough crisis point for me to realise that I had to seriously step in before it got significantly worse ...

Chapter 11

Nile Wilson – The Tough Times

This particular call from Nile made it crystal clear to me that things needed to change. And very quickly.

It was Saturday, 26 August 2019, and Nile had been at the England versus Australia Test match at Headingley all day with his dad and sister. I actually knew what to expect before I made the call as his sister, Joanna, had texted me.

'Nile and dad have had a huge fight. It's awful. They are both drunk.'

And I knew this was brewing. Nile's behaviour had been getting more and more erratic, and although there were spells when I thought we were making progress, the reality was that it had been a gradual decline. His family, no one more than his father Neil, had found this so hard to watch. Frustration and even some anger were bubbling up. Headingley was like the perfect storm.

I called Nile and he was indeed very drunk, and also distressed. He had argued badly with his dad about his behaviour that day. He was upset and sounded confused and desperate. I had once been in Nile's shoes, so had experience of how to handle this. Trying to reason with someone so drunk and emotional was a fool's errand. I tried to calm him and told him I loved him and supported him. I begged him to look after himself that night and said I would come to his apartment as soon as I could the next day. I knew when I put down the phone that his night of drinking hadn't finished but there was nothing that could be done until tomorrow.

Deep down, I knew this moment was coming. The last few months had been so difficult for Nile and everyone around him. He had suffered some really bad injuries and his mental health had deteriorated but no one had come up with any real way to deal with it all. He was also trapped in this pressure cooker of feeling he needed to live up to being 'Nile'. It was not a good mix. With that, his behaviour, particularly with alcohol, became worse. And with that behaviour, his mental health continued to slide. It was a vicious cycle to be in.

Everyone wanted to help him and that group included his family, me, his coaches, doctor and physiotherapist. We had been talking about it increasingly amongst ourselves. The greatest challenge with identifying someone with mental health issues and then helping them is that the symptoms don't just roar at you in a split second. It is all very gradual. Nile's deterioration had been over twelve months, not twelve days. And during this time, there had been periods when he seemed to bounce back. It was just that the 'Fuck It' button, as I call it, was never far away from his reach.

I had felt everything Nile was feeling and had made all the same mistakes. I had once been as confused and lonely in my own head as he now was in his. He didn't need to be shamed out of it. It wouldn't work. Deep down, he already felt ashamed of himself. He needed understanding, which included some tough talking, but most importantly, he needed to identify with someone else's experience and then be signposted towards solutions rather than the 'Fuck It' button. Sorry, I should have explained the 'Fuck It' button: it's the metaphorical button we press when we decide we are not going to deal with reality and get smashed out of our heads instead. NB: the 'Fuck It' button never leads to good things!

Nile had gone from being the most brilliantly creative, charismatic, productive, entertaining, loving and fun person to be around, to someone who became nervous when leaving his apartment and was constantly tired, burdened with pressure and suffocated by his issues. It felt like a night out with his friends was never far away, and when it started, no one was quite sure when it would finish. His family found this really difficult to deal with. They didn't like what they saw and wanted their Nile back. The more they tried, the further he seemed to slip away. In their hurt and confusion, they would use harsh words with him to get him to 'snap out of it'. It was all done out of pure love, and we have all been guilty of it at times when we wanted someone we love to do something better with their lives. But shaming Nile only compounded things, and during this night in Headingley, the situation reached a crescendo. Things needed to change.

I arrived at Nile's apartment the following day about 4.00 pm. I couldn't get there any earlier, but I also knew this wasn't a bad time to arrive. The morning was a write-off and he needed a few hours in the afternoon for the hangover to really kick in, in order for him to really listen to what needed to be said. As he opened the door he looked awful – pale and nervous, not the exuberant Olympic athlete that was truly him. He was hung-over to hell.

I did my best to greet him as if he looked a million dollars. I could see the shame in his face, and he was totally aware of how he appeared. I didn't want him to think I was judging him, and that was the truth; I wasn't judging him at all. I had been in his place many times and he needed help and guidance.

We made a coffee and sat on his balcony. I wanted him to talk. It was important he told me exactly how he was feeling, not what he thought I wanted to hear. Of course, I knew he had been struggling with depression and, particularly, anxiety of late, and that his drinking was not in a healthy place, but all of that was the end product of some disconnected thinking. I needed to understand where his thinking was currently at. Why did he think he felt the way he did? Why did he think that he had argued with his dad the day before? What did he think about his relationship with alcohol?

He explained how lost he felt. He didn't really understand it but it seemed he had lost all joy in anything other than going out and drinking. He didn't really know who he was any more or what made him happy. He was sad about how much his behaviour was upsetting his family, but he felt they just didn't understand. They didn't understand what a dark place he was in and that drinking was his only saviour. I could hear the confusion and pain in him. I knew it well. I had been in that very same mental place. It's excruciatingly lonely. And that loneliness doesn't come from not having people around you. Nile had lots of people around him, including me. It is the loneliness inside your own head. You feel ashamed with yourself that you feel the way you do and that you are acting the way you are.

This wasn't the first time we had talked about all of this, but maybe it was the first time we had talked *exactly* like this. Maybe it was the window we had to help make change in his life. We decided to walk into Leeds and get some food. As we walked and then ate, I talked about my experiences in rehab and dealing with my own demons. I explained to him that I completely understood where he was coming from and there was a way out of it, but it involved change – significant change. Nile immediately assumed that this change meant making sure he didn't go out or change his routine, and I explained that those things would help, but on their own they definitely wouldn't solve his problems. I told him that if he wanted to drink, he would, regardless of what I or anyone else said or did, and that the change had to come from within him.

First and foremost, he needed to initiate his own actions and decisions. He had to take responsibility for how he was dealing with his mental health. Yes, he was escaping that pain through drinking, and when it started, he struggled to stop, but that was a choice. His mental health challenges were not a choice, but doing everything he could to overcome them and create a good mental space in his life were 100 per cent his choice. So often, someone experiencing these difficulties finds it very difficult to make sense of the solutions. They are stuck in the problem and the blame for that problem, e.g. 'My mental health is poor because of my injury, so, because of that, I drink a lot and that makes my mental health worse, so I drink even more' … and so on, and so on. It almost sounds like it is inevitable, with no solution in sight.

But that's not true. It is about owning your decisions. If you want to go out drinking, then own it. Know it is your choice to do so and understand what comes with it. Don't believe that there is nothing you can do about it. If you don't want to train that day and choose not to, then own it. It is your choice, so live with it. I explained to Nile that the time when I started to make real changes in my life was when I stopped looking for reasons to explain my actions and started owning all the decisions I was making. Suddenly it was ALL my responsibility. It is a subtle shift, but it definitely makes a significant change. As mental health issues often creep in slowly, the solutions can take time to materialise. Someone has to commit to finding better ways of dealing with the mental space they are in. It involves a certain amount of humility to ask for help as well as commitment to know that there is not an overnight fix.

Nile is a truly exceptional person, but he had slipped into a self-destructive cycle. His search for a way out of it was being led by some misplaced thinking, which led to more problems. As we chatted, I could see in his eyes that he sensed there was a different way of doing this. I explained to him that I also wanted him to explore what he felt his purpose on the earth was. He was trapped in a world of views, likes, followers and subscribers that had all been created by his own success. But he was finding that that wasn't a real measure of his happiness. He was achieving great numbers but not achieving great happiness. So, I challenged him with this thought of having a bigger purpose to his life. Something that was real and measurable at any given moment of the day. I had heard Nile talk so many times about 'loving the journey', which, in essence, was his way of explaining that we need to enjoy the process of what we are doing, not focus on the end result. In gymnastics terms, enjoy the experience of training and mastering a skill, and not be too hung up on whether you are going to win a gold medal or not. But throughout this time, he had lost this perspective. He was fixated on quick-fix solutions for his emotional state – a night out, some new clothes, a vlog that might go viral – anything except something deep within him that gave him true happiness. He didn't know where to look any more.

I felt like this time together was a real turning point for Nile, but it was only a start. He was hung-over, vulnerable and very willing to listen. The challenges would come again when he went back to normal life. I pointed out to him that there was so much more to do, and we both knew that we needed more time together. Nile and I have always been extremely close, but it was at times like this that we felt like brothers. His issues were exactly the issues I had had. I was twenty years older than him and had come out the other side. I felt like he really needed me. As with my time with James Taylor, this was a moment in my management career when it felt real and meaningful.

Nile and I eventually decided to have a week away in mine and my fiancée's house in Ibiza. Nile had only ever associated Ibiza with partying, but this was going to be very different! As much as anything, it was just an opportunity to spend lots of time together and chat through where he was at in his life. We had a little routine every day that involved one or all of – a trip to the gym (he trained, I drank coffee), a self-awareness session, a meditation session and a pool session (again, I watched). We were like a little married couple pottering around Ibiza! Nile also got to spend time with my family as well as lots of sleep and good food. It was absolutely brilliant.

I wanted to continue all the themes we had talked about in England but get him to really dig deep. My aim was to give him enough guidance to come away from the week with a feeling of hope and an understanding of how he wanted to live the rest of his life. I hoped he would begin to discover that purpose in his life that was always attached to the true Nile. Everything we did and talked about was everything I had learned in recovering from my issues.

We looked at how he defined himself – asking the question how he identified whether he was doing well in the world and as a human being. It was clear that, at that point in time, almost everything was attached to achievement. That was why being injured had such an enormous impact on him. Of course, injury affects every elite athlete, but not all of them press the 'Fuck It' button! If Nile was injured, then he couldn't achieve things in gymnastics, and this had a profound impact on his self-worth and purpose. When he was injured, the success he was used to was not accessible to him, so he felt entirely lost.

The only substitute he had was everything he was achieving online, but none of that felt real or had the same impact as success in his sport when he was fit. It was like a drug with an ever-depreciating effect on him. As that started to give him little sense of worth, he was left in a really dangerous place. His only answer was to reach out for quick fixes like a big night out. Nile recognised and understood this. He began to realise that he wanted to be defined by the type of person he is by his family, friends and supporters. Of course, he still wanted to win multiple Olympic gold medals and become a multi-millionaire, but those achievements would not ultimately define him. As with all this stuff, it was a subtle shift in focus that made for a profound change in him. It meant that if he was injured, he wouldn't experience an enormous lack of self-worth, because his purpose in life encompassed much more than that. He would feel sad and desperately disappointed, but not completely defeated by it.

So, we moved our talks on to how he would nourish this sense of purpose in his life. He understood that it wasn't something to take for granted, it had to be nurtured. He should be careful about what he did and who he hung around with. He needed to learn to live his life from the heart rather than from the ego, and to constantly work on himself to be able to grow and protect what was important and good for him in his life.

That week we had in Ibiza was actually as mind-blowing for me as much as it was for him. We made such big progress, and although I knew that these sorts of issues can come around to bite you when you least expect it, it felt like Nile had an anchor for himself. An anchor to the person he wanted to be.

In many ways, Nile has never looked back since then. He is growing and developing all the time, but most importantly, he is back enjoying life and his gymnastics. He has found his happiness.

We recently released his documentary, *The Silent Battle*, on his YouTube channel, which was an amazing bit of work to show the journey Nile has been on.

Nile is truly capable of anything. As we move to a 2021 Olympics, it wouldn't surprise me to see Nile win a gold medal, and then take himself and gymnastics to a level no one can quite imagine right now.

There are very few sportspeople like Nile Wilson, and it would be dangerous to ever underestimate what he is capable of achieving, both in and out of the gymnastics arena.

Chapter 12

Does Sport Have a Problem with Racism?

Does professional sport have an issue with racism?

Yes.

That question is actually a multi-layered one within sport and my answer can be pointed at a number of different areas within the industry. The easiest area to place it is within fan behaviour. In the last year, we have seen yet more racist incidents within football and Jofra Archer being racially abused by a fan while walking off the cricket field in New Zealand.

But solely laying this issue at the feet of the fans is simply not good enough. I want to give you a fuller perspective from within professional sport.

What we witness in fan behaviour is simply the head of the snake. The issue of racism has been there in professional sport, and society, for that matter, for a very long time. We went through a period where racist behaviour was deemed socially unacceptable, but now, not so much ... so we see more. However, whether or not we have witnessed obvious racist behaviour, the underlying issues have always been there.

Sol Campbell's battle to even get into football management, let alone to rise within it having done brilliantly at his first club, Macclesfield Town, is a stark difference to the opportunities that have been afforded to ex-players of similar reputation like Steven Gerrard and Frank Lampard. Taking into consideration there are so few black managers within top-flight football in this country, no one can truly rule out the fact that racism has played a part. Without more black role models in football management, it gives aspiring black managers little encouragement that they can make the climb. You then get fewer people of colour trying to become football managers and the whole thing is in a negative cycle.

It is an uncomfortable reality for people to face up to, but racial prejudice exists within all sport. I have managed a number of Asian cricketers, some playing for England, some for India and some for Pakistan. I have also played against or alongside a number of Asian cricketers. In my mind, there is no question that these players face an element of racial prejudice all the time. Let us take the Pakistani players as an example. Sadly, the Pakistan cricket team has been embroiled in high-profile instances of match-fixing and ball-tampering in fairly recent history. In fact, one player whom I managed, Mohammed Amir, was front and centre of the match-fixing scandal in 2010 and was eventually banned from all cricket for five years. The tarnish of these scandals has 100 per cent affected how all Pakistani players are viewed and treated within cricket. As soon as a Pakistani batsman scores too slowly during a crucial period of a one-day game, or gets out in a ridiculous fashion, the immediate reaction is, 'Well, I guess he was on the take', meaning, we are presuming the player was being paid to perform badly as part of a match-fixing scam. As soon as Pakistani bowlers get the ball to reverse swing, the immediate reaction is, 'They will have been tampering with the ball', meaning, they have cheated to get an unfair advantage. You might ask where those reactions come from. Well, it was definitely in teams I played in, it was definitely in pubs I watched cricket in, and it has definitely been in an undercurrent of some media reporting. You might argue that this is just the unfortunate consequence for the players of a team that has been involved in such scandals. But then you may be forgetting something very important …

Other national teams have been involved in these sorts of scandals.

In fact, other national teams have been involved in these sorts of scandals more recently than the Pakistan team. When the Australian cricketers David Warner and Cameron Bancroft were found guilty of ball-tampering when playing South Africa in an extraordinary scandal, the cricket world went mad. Both players, plus the captain, Steven Smith, were widely condemned and then banned. But now, nearly two years on, ball-tampering is not something that sticks reputationally to Australian players. Not even slightly. And all three players are playing again. Indeed, the South Africa captain, Faf du Plessis, one of cricket's best people, has been found guilty of ball-tampering not once, but twice, yet it is not something that sticks to the South African cricket team. So why in some cases is it an individual's problem or mistake and in another case it is a cultural issue of a nation's team? We have to be asking these sorts of uncomfortable questions.

In 2006, on the fourth day of the Test match between England and Pakistan at The Oval, the umpires Darrell Hair and Billy Doctrove ruled that Pakistan had been ball-tampering. In protest to the decision, Pakistan refused to take to the field after the tea break. The umpires waited and then declared England winner by forfeiture. This was the first such end to a Test match in over a thousand tests. The match referee later acquitted Pakistan captain Inzamam-ul-Haq of a ball-tampering charge, but the stain of the incident stuck with Pakistan for a long time. This was on two fronts: everyone presumed they were guilty because that was their 'reputation'; and people objected to their refusal to return to the field in protest. But take a minute to compare this with how England were treated by fans and media over the fact that they famously used mints to help them shine the ball, *only a year earlier*, in winning the Ashes in 2005. It could easily be argued that that was a form of ball-tampering, but England weren't shamed for it and there definitely hasn't been any long-lasting reputational damage for the team. No wonder Pakistan were infuriated by the charge being levelled against them and would have felt they were being singled out. If we were honest, we might just have to consider there is racial prejudice at play again.

Match or spot-fixing scandals are not exclusive to Asian cricket teams. Once upon a time, Mark Waugh and Shane Warne were found guilty of giving bookmakers team news in exchange for money. Mark Waugh subsequently became a national selector. A brief search of cricketers banned for corruption will show you that there are players from England, South Africa, New Zealand, West Indies and Kenya. Granted, the highest numbers of players banned are from Asian countries, and illegal betting is a huge issue in those countries, but to imply that the Pakistan team has a cultural issue with cheating is placing a racial slant on it. We fail to appreciate the enormous burden that most Pakistani cricketers carry in having to support their immediate and extended family. They are not paid as well as most other national team players, so the pressure on them is huge at times. They are clearly going to be a target for illegal bookmakers, so it is no wonder there are more players from Asia banned than other areas of the world – but that doesn't mean it is a cultural issue. I played in a Lancashire team in which Lou Vincent from New Zealand admitted to spot-fixing while he was playing for us. He even admitted to trying to recruit other players during that time. I didn't have a clue what he was doing and wasn't ever approached, but I can absolutely say that there was no cultural issue of match or spot-fixing at Lancashire. We just happened to have a teammate who had got himself into some serious trouble. There is no question that there are double standards in cricket when it comes to the Asian teams, mainly Pakistan, and the rest of the world.

I can give another example of the unfair perception that Asian cricketers and teams are more disposed to cheating or corruption. Asian teams can appeal a lot to the umpire. That's a fact. It is born from playing cricket in spin-friendly conditions in which there are lots of fielders close to the bat looking for catches. Those conditions mean there are lots of chances of getting people out and, therefore, lots of appeals. As a result, an impression or narrative has been created over the years that Asian teams cheat a lot because they are appealing for things they know are probably not out. But compare this with other teams – remember Stuart Broad not walking when he edged the ball to first slip in the Ashes versus Australia in 2013? In fact, remember a multitude of appeals when they knew it probably wasn't out and batsmen not walking when they knew they were out from countless cricketers from England, Australia, South Africa, New Zealand and the West Indies? It goes on all the time. And is done by everyone! Yet the narrative is spun that Asian teams cheat more. It just isn't true. I'll repeat what I said earlier: for some it is considered an individual's error, but for others it is considered a deep cultural issue. That can only be a form of racial prejudice.

There is an enormous Asian cricket-playing community in England but only a comparatively tiny number of Asian players at the highest level. I appreciate that work has been done by the ECB to try to help engage these communities better, but we also have to be honest in assessing why this issue exists. Young Asian cricketers don't see many leaders or role models for them within cricket. They also see a difficult path for them to grow through the sport, and why is that? Traditional Asian families are culturally different to the vast majority of traditional white English families. That is a fact we so often fail to even try to understand. Religion, family and their cricket can be, by some distance, the biggest three things in their lives. As a result, they can approach their cricket and everything around it in a different manner to the way in which the average white English family will. Look back over the last few years at some of the Asian England cricketers who at some point got labelled 'difficult' – Adil Rashid, Samit Patel, Ajmal Shahzad, Haseeb Hameed, Monty Panesar and now, quite possibly, Moeen Ali. These guys have been or are the role models for the Asian cricket-playing communities in this country and yet there seems to have been a problem with all of them at some point. If you were an aspiring cricketer from an Asian community in England, then this wouldn't be terribly encouraging. So, why are there issues? In my opinion, it is because these guys approach their careers from exactly the basis I have described from their family base. Their absolute priorities are their religion, family and cricket; and, as a result, they won't buy into anything that compromises those things. Don't get me wrong, this can exist amongst non-Asian players as well, but there seems to be a strength and intensity around this for Asian cricketers that some people find very uncomfortable.

Haseeb Hameed is a good example of this. I have never seen anyone practise as much as him. He and his father were relentless. Haseeb wouldn't necessarily be relaxing the way other players would be, for example, with a game of cards or some silly chat about *Love Island*, and he most definitely would not be going on a night out after a game. His religion and upbringing would not allow this and all he would really want to do was practise and play cricket. As a result, he would be an immediate outlier in the team. He also only cared about his cricket career, so if something happened in the team with a decision that didn't suit him then he would never be able to see it any other way than that this was totally unacceptable for him. It wasn't because he was a bad person; in fact, Haseeb is a great guy. It was because of his upbringing and family base. Yet, so often in this country, we don't look to understand these key dynamics and simply label the player as 'difficult'. All that does is to send out a really poor message to the Asian community of 'you need to fit in with us'. Although this is not overtly racist as such, it does seed an attitude and an approach that causes a racial divide within cricket.

All of this creates a lack of leadership within sport for people of colour. A distinct lack of role models for their colour not only sends a dispiriting message to them but also sends a message to the ignorant wider sporting environment that people of colour are of less serious standing. Ask yourself, when will we see a black person as the England football manager? Likewise, when will we see an Asian person as England Cricket's head coach? I couldn't sit here and say that it will be within my lifetime. Yet, picture this scenario: England have just won the football World Cup. It has finally come home! There is dancing in the streets as the nation celebrates our biggest prize in sport. The players are labelled as national heroes and the manager is seen as a sporting genius. And then, add to this scene one more thing ... the manager is black. Do you think that there would be more or fewer racist attacks on black players in the Premier League if this was the case? There would undoubtedly be fewer. Black players, black managers, black people would be taken far more seriously and seen less as easy targets for some ignorant racist chant. This is an uncomfortable reality for us to face up to, but it is right there in front of us.

Lewis Hamilton has won six World Championships and will be a true great of Formula 1 – incidentally, a sport dominated by white people. Yet, despite six world titles, Lewis is largely uncelebrated by the wider British public. Motor sport fans rightly speak out for what a remarkable driver and ambassador he is for the sport, but why is he so unappreciated at this point in time? Some argue that it is because he doesn't seem that 'English'; he lives overseas for tax reasons and is more likely to be seen at Paris Fashion Week than in a pub watching his football team play. I would argue that those things have played their part but if I remember correctly, Jenson Button has also lived overseas for tax reasons. Andy Murray even once said he would support any nation over England that was playing them at football because he felt so strongly about being Scottish. So, why after six World Championships does Hamilton still battle for recognition and support from British sports fans beyond motor sport? I'm not sure we will ever know the answer to that, but the question is: can we rule out an element of racism within this? I don't think we can.

What are the solutions – particularly from my point of view as a sports agent?

We have had various campaigns over the years supported by some extremely high-profile athletes to spell out that racism is always unacceptable in sport. These campaigns are well-meaning and look great but, let's face it, they are simply not working. Racism hasn't got better in recent times; in fact, it has got much worse. Arguably this is because of a wider issue within society, and I am not arguing against that, but we have to do more within sport itself. The campaigns make us feel better, but they don't cut through to the deep underlying issues of prejudice we face. In my opinion, anyone involved in sport, including sports agents, who truly wants to help this situation, needs to encourage and work to get people of colour in the most senior positions of professional sport. The lack of role models is a major issue holding back progress being made in getting rid of racial prejudice. The fan who shouts monkey noises at a black player does so through ignorance and a lack of respect for black people. That fan already knows that what he or she is doing is socially unacceptable, yet still does it. It's not enough. Punishments and sanctions warn people off doing it, but only for a period of time. The underlying issues are still there. The true way to combat this is to have people of colour in positions within sport that makes that fan respect them and anyone else of colour.

Within my job, this is about supporting clients of colour as best I can. This can be in helping bridge the gap between the cultural difference between a player and his or her family and the club they are playing for. It could also involve supporting them if they want to leave the sporting field due to racial abuse. This step needs to happen at some point soon. It would cause an enormous storm in this country, especially if it was during a Premier League football match. But big actions are going to have to be taken to force change, and I would wholeheartedly support a client if they felt they wanted to do this.

For clients of colour coming to the end of their career, this would be about me encouraging them to go for head coach and managerial positions when they finish playing, and fighting the cause for them. I think sport needs to work together from within to solve these problems. Overcoming the denial of the full extent of racial prejudice that lies within sport is the first step to achieving this, but the true answers come from everyone working from within, and not just labelling the idiotic fan displaying racist behaviour in the stands as an isolated incident.

Chapter 13

The Impact of Covid-19 on the Sports Industry

2020 – the year of Covid-19. We are not going to forget this one! Trying to describe the impact Covid-19 has had on everyone's lives seems pretty pointless other than to say it has been massive. The whole world basically came to standstill.

The sports industry was no different and the effects were felt through every level of it. It was completely unprecedented in my lifetime and, as an agent, it threw up lots of challenges.

People don't tend to have much sympathy with well-paid professional sportspeople, but this situation was extremely difficult for them. For the Olympians, they were nearing the end of a four-year cycle of enormous dedication to then be told the Games were postponed. For cricketers, their entire season looked like it would be wiped out; and for footballers on the verge of enormously important title-winning matches or relegation battles, everything was placed on hold.

Of course, sport isn't life or death, but for professional sportspeople, these dynamics have been very hard on their mental well-being. Their sport is not just their job; it is their identity. For a small few, they will have more outside of sport, but for the vast majority, they will eat, live and breathe their sport. They will be consumed by achieving more and improving their skills. To suddenly have a situation where this is completely stopped and out of their hands was extremely hard for them.

Suddenly, there are no contests and not even any meaningful training for people conditioned from a very early age that this is their focus in life. They are competitors, and if they don't have that, then what do they do? Many of them felt lost.

Professional sportspeople are often perceived to live a privileged life and, for the ones earning significant amounts of money, that is true in some ways. But they are also human beings, and throughout the Covid-19 crisis, the responsibility of agents, teams and governing bodies to check on the mental well-being of players was very important.

With regards to the commercial side of things, other than a few exceptions, it basically ground to a halt. Sponsors had a situation that meant their businesses were under enormous strain and they were now not going to get any value from their sponsorship as there were no competitions to link it to. The only exceptions to this were companies that were still allowed to trade fully during Covid-19, and particularly ones that based their entire offering online.

Within the first two weeks of the pandemic, taking a grip on everything, I received half a dozen requests from sponsors to pause contractual arrangements with certain clients. Everybody was understanding, and there was never an issue over this. It felt like everything was a pack of cards and if anyone was unreasonable and pushed too hard, then everything and everyone would come toppling down. It was very much a situation that we were 'all in it together'. There were very few examples of businesses not being owed money but also not owing money themselves. Everyone needed to be patient with each other. Suddenly, the dog–eat–dog commercial world of the sports industry became more understanding of the web that we were all caught in. I actually received an email from one Team GB sponsor, who was not as badly affected by the situation as others, to inform me that they would reduce their payment terms from thirty days to seven days because they realised how difficult a situation it was for everyone. It was an amazing gesture that I have never seen happen before.

Like the whole world, I do hope the sports industry learns from what Covid-19 brought. The spirit of collaboration and understanding needs to continue. I'm not naïve enough to believe that that will happen 100 per cent, but I hope some of it still exists in the way people deal with each other. Suddenly, an industry so bulletproof and wealthy felt extremely fragile.

Nonetheless, the reality is that the sports industry is going to have to be more collaborative going forward. They will have no choice with the postponements that have been caused by pushing so much out of 2020, and 2021 will see the biggest pile-up of sporting events we have ever seen.

As you read this you will likely think this point concentrates on the scheduling of the major events such as the Olympic Games in Tokyo, football's European Championships, Wimbledon and the Open. But the pile-up for 2021 caused by the coronavirus is actually much more subtle than just those events. For example, and by no means an isolated case, at the moment, the World Swimming Championships are scheduled for 16 July to 1 August 2021 in Fukuoka, Japan. Yet those dates cross over with the rearranged Olympics in the same country. The Games are now set for a start date of 23 July and a finish of 8 August.

There has been talk that FINA, swimming's world governing body, would hold the World Championships just after the Olympics. It means that for the likes of, among others, Britain's Adam Peaty, the pursuit of peaking for the two biggest events in the sport at almost the same time, which is actually impossible.

But this is only part of the picture. For an athlete to qualify for major events, they need to take part in enough domestic or international qualifying events. Take gymnastics, where a competitor can qualify for the Olympics via their results in the numerous World Cup series throughout a year. These events have been severely disrupted and are likely to be cancelled for the remainder of 2020, so they will need to be fitted into whatever time is available in 2021 alongside a European Championships in March and further domestic qualifying events.

Also consider that, ordinarily, a gymnast would want a minimum of an eight-week window to prepare for a major competition. There is no way around it: it will be a logistical nightmare for athletes, coaches and organisers.

This doesn't just affect athletes and sports, because broadcasters, too, are going to have a massive challenge. Next summer, the BBC will be showing Men's Football Euros, Wimbledon, the Tokyo Olympics and the Women's Football Euros. The cancellations mean an enormous challenge of reorganisation, with the additional tournaments factored to give every event the attention it deserves.

Sponsors and advertisers will also face their challenges within this. They will all want their value for money of the advertising space or activity they have paid for before, during and after a major event. Ordinarily, this needs a certain amount of space to grab the attention they want. With so much going on all at the same time, this will be very tough, possibly even impossible. There could easily be a situation where two sponsors collaborate to help each other.

Whichever way you look at it, 2021 is going to have to see an unprecedented amount of collaboration between sports, broadcasters, sponsors and teams. They have no choice. If they all fight for dominance, it will be a mess. They are going to have to help each other and even share resources at times.

I guess the question that everyone is asking in every industry is whether all these enforced changes will reshape the way we operate forever.

Sadly, I don't think it will. The sports industry is enormously valuable. Live sport still holds one of the greatest premiums for advertisers. In an age of viewing on demand, live sport is one of the rare things that will make people set aside time to watch. If you are a football fan living in Manchester and United are playing City, then you will do nothing else other than try to watch that derby from kick-off. For advertisers, this is golden, so the industry will always be awash with money, nowhere more so than the Premier League. With money like that around, people will sadly soon go back to protecting their territory and trying to steal that of others. Dog eat dog will be back soon enough, unfortunately.

Similar to the way that the narrative of all agents being rotten to the core is used by various people for less than honourable reasons, I think the same could be said about how Premier League footballers and their apparent lack of touch with the common man was used during Covid-19.

Health Secretary Matt Hancock singled out Premier League footballers during a Covid-19 press conference as people who should take a cut in wages during this time. By putting a spotlight on them, there was a presumption that they wouldn't be doing this unless forced or that they weren't already giving any thought to how they could help the NHS and others during this crisis. It was really poor, and in the same speech there was no mention of other highly paid sportspeople, or other millionaires or even the billionaires in the country. Football was being used as a convenient focal point within a PR spin.

As I've said earlier in this book, the truth is that football lost its working-class soul a very long time ago. The disconnection between the heart of its fans and the business of the sport has never been greater. But that doesn't mean the vast majority of players have lost any sense of their community and their position of privilege.

Matches are watched by thousands in the stadium and millions on the TV who couldn't imagine what it is like to earn the sums of money the players on the field do. Their lives seem a sort of far-off dream. The players have become unreachable humans who are just observed from afar, and the clubs owned by people with mind-blowing wealth. Then there are the prices of season tickets, merchandise, home and away kits, TV subscriptions, travel … and on it goes, with the average football fan feeding the bloated game. But that is the market that the players work in. They didn't create that market.

The early news that Newcastle, Tottenham and Liverpool had furloughed non-playing staff without asking players to take a wage cut was seized upon by many, and both clubs – owned by billionaires – were lambasted. But, again, this wasn't the players' decision. The reaction was premature as it presumed that the players were not going to do anything. Matt Hancock's comments only helped to enflame negative feelings towards players. Yet the reality of the situation wasn't straightforward. A wage cut for players could arguably fall straight back into the hands of the billionaire owners. Instead, many players were looking for a way for a cut in their wages to be directly donated to NHS causes. This needed agreement from players and executives at the club. It would all take a little bit of time.

In the end, Premier League footballers across the country stood up and made enormously generous contributions to the NHS and other causes desperately needing help during the pandemic. The vast majority of Premier League footballers are very aware of their working-class roots and how incredibly fortunate they are. They were always going to act. People should not have confused the disconnection of the business of football from our working-class communities with the players themselves. People should also take note how a narrative was used against footballers for selfish reasons. Just remember what I said about how it is used with agents in a similar way. It has been done many times and will happen again.

Marcus Rashford then underlined this point better than anyone possibly could. Not only did he embarrass the government but also anyone else who wants to spin the narrative that footballers don't care about those less privileged than themselves.

Back on 19 March 2020, Rashford first went on social media to highlight his fears about the impact that shutting schools would have on disadvantaged children. Rashford is, remarkably, still only 22 years old, and it is only eleven years since the Manchester United and England striker needed breakfast clubs and free school meals to supplement what his mum could provide. She was the head of a single-parent family of five children, working full-time on the minimum wage.

When, on 18 March, Prime Minister Boris Johnson told the country that schools had to help combat the spread of Covid-19, Rashford immediately knew what that would mean. While most parents wondered how they were going to manage childcare, Rashford wondered how kids who were growing up as he had would get fed.

'Guys, across the UK there are over 32,000 schools. Tomorrow all of these will close. Many of the children attending these schools rely on free meals, so I've spent the last few days talking to organisations to understand how this deficit is going to be filled,' Rashford wrote on social media.

In just under thirteen weeks, Rashford had helped supply the equivalent of three million meals. He had highlighted the damage caused by the 'invisible issue of food insecurity'. He received messages of support from clubs and organisations across the country. And, crucially, he had changed government policy. Boris Johnson was forced into a U-turn over providing food vouchers for some of England's poorest families after the pressure imposed by Rashford's campaign. That is truly extraordinary, and, I will say it again – Marcus Rashford is 22 years old.

In Rashford's open letter to MPs, he summed up how acutely he remembers his upbringing:

As a family, we relied on breakfast clubs, free school meals, and the kind actions of neighbours and coaches. Food banks and soup kitchens were not alien to us; I recall very clearly our visits to Northern Moor to collect our Christmas dinners every year. It's only now that I really understand the enormous sacrifice my mum made in sending me away to live in digs aged 11, a decision no mother would ever make lightly.

Football may have lost its working-class soul, but don't believe for one moment that that includes the vast majority of the players.

Chapter 14

What Makes a Great Agent?

W hat makes a great sports agent?
It's a bloody good question and, as ever, it depends what you consider a success. So, I guess I should start by giving my opinion of what I think a great sports agent looks like.

Clearly, monetary success is one of the easiest benchmarks to measure and there is no question that successful agents are ones who have helped contribute to increased earnings for their clients. However, I would argue that this is a byproduct of a client being happy, professional and stable, and being given the correct opportunities. For example, Cristiano Ronaldo has become the world's richest footballer, but playing the way he has was always going to result in him being an extraordinarily well-paid player. So should we be congratulating the agent for the contracts he has secured or that he has helped keep Ronaldo on a stable footing that has led him to play the best football he can? The answer is both, but I would argue the latter is more important. The only significant caveat to this is the part about clients being given the correct opportunities. Talented players in any sport need to be noticed and this isn't easy in such a competitive world. Some catch a break early and get spotted by the media or someone influential in their sport, but the majority need someone to fight their corner so their talents are recognised. That's the same for Ronaldo or anyone else. An agent has to be good at this in order to give their player the platform from which to explode. The agent needs good contacts but, most importantly, he/she needs credibility. They need people to listen to them when they tell them someone is good.

I think there is a broader perspective on whether an agent has increased a client's earnings. If you are one of the world's best at your particular sport, then you will attract all the best sponsors from that sport. You are within your own bubble and will earn as well from that as pretty much possible. But the really good agents are the ones who can secure commercial partners for a sportsperson outside of their immediate sport bubble. The pinnacle of this is obviously David Beckham – an excellent footballer but a personality who has attracted sponsors or commercial partners from all categories. He is absolutely not limited to anything related to football. Don't underestimate the role his management and PR team have played in this over the years. The key question to examine whether someone has been able to achieve this is, 'Does the average housewife know who they are?' Beckham gets an overwhelming 'Yes' to this question!

A more tangible example of this is Tom Daley. Tom is one of our biggest sporting stars, with a ton of charisma and personality. But Tom also does a niche sport in diving, which only really hits the mainstream media headlines every four years with the Olympics. Tom has very successfully managed to stretch far beyond the diving world, but also beyond the sporting bubble. His commercial partners include many lifestyle brands, which means his image and appeal are being used to advertise beyond the sporting world. This is an example of how Tom and his management have handled his career very successfully to date. An example of the opposite of this would be someone like Steven Gerrard. He is one of the best footballers this country has ever produced, and a legend in Liverpool, but his commercial appeal didn't stretch far beyond football. As I understand it, he didn't particularly want to search for commercial value in the same way that Beckham did, but I am sure he wouldn't have argued with it if it had landed in his lap. And that's the point: it doesn't land in your lap! To go beyond your sport on a commercial level takes careful management and commitment from the client to trust the agent's lead in how to do this.

My best personal examples would be Sam Quek, Jimmy Anderson and Nile Wilson, whom have I have already spoken about at length throughout this book. All three of them, in very different ways, have been able to stretch their appeal beyond their sports. In Sam and Nile's cases, this is even more remarkable because their sports are so niche.

So, if you are looking for an excellent agent, look for someone who is able to help their clients earn more money by broadening their appeal beyond their original bubble.

However, I want to go back to stability. It is a big one for me. I believe that talented sportspeople will eventually shine through if they are given the correct environment, and the key to that is stability. So, if you are looking at whether an agent is successful, look for the calibre of his or her clients, but also look for how stable that group is. I don't mean whether clients in that group aren't in trouble or having difficulties; unfortunately, there are many things beyond the control of an agent. I mean stability around whether clients are coming or going. If there is a high turnover rate, then something isn't quite right. If an agent is holding on to most of their clients for five years or more then it means they are doing a lot right.

I have previously mentioned the cricket agent Neil Fairbrother, and I think he is a wonderful example of what I am talking about here. Neil manages or has managed two of the biggest stars in cricket at their absolute peak – Andrew Flintoff and Ben Stokes. Both of them were/are extraordinary cricketers, massive characters and not without their troubles off the field. Throughout their careers, Neil has been a rock for them, providing that stability that they could always come back to. In 2019, Ben Stokes went from nearly being jailed for affray to winning the World Cup and playing mind-blowingly brilliantly in the Ashes for England. There is a huge story of resurrection behind all of that, and Neil played a massive role in it. There is no question that Ben Stokes's life was at a crossroads while he stood in that court in Bristol, and to come back from that says an awful lot about Ben, his family, his friends and … his agent.

When Ben scored the runs to win the Ashes Test match for England at Headingley in the greatest innings I have ever seen, I thought of

Neil and dropped him a message to congratulate him. Neil was happily under the radar, and very few would have considered him right then and there, but I am absolutely certain that Ben didn't underestimate the role he played in his life.

I have highlighted some aspects of what I believe makes an excellent agent, but the next question would be, 'What personal characteristics does an agent need to have to achieve these things?' This might help anyone reading who one day wants to move into sports management. So here we go …

You need to be organised: You're going to be managing the diaries of multiple people!

You need to be good with people: You're going to be managing clients, their families, their friends, sponsors, clubs, the media etc., so if you are not good with people, then don't bother.

You need to always be well prepared: Research everything – the sports, people, brands and everything in between that you work with.

You need to be creative: Every week, sometimes every day, will throw up problems for you, so you have to be able to find solutions for things, and quickly. Creativity is vital!

You need to understand marketing: The best don't wait for commercial deals to arrive; they know what the markets are looking for and position their clients accordingly.

You need to understand the media: Respect the media, you need them.

You need to be willing to reach out for help: You are not going to know or be able to manage everything involved with managing a big client. You are the ultimate middleman, but you also need to be in the middle of a group of very good people helping you.

Having discussed what makes a good agent, it is probably worth me covering what I think makes for a bad agent. And when I say 'bad', I am not just talking about someone who doesn't have the attributes that I have listed above; I think that would just make an incompetent agent. I am talking about someone much worse than that.

Beware of agents who push themselves to the front when things are going well.

Sadly, there are agents who believe it is all about them. When times are good, they want everyone to know about the role they are playing; and when times are bad, they simply disappear. In my opinion, these guys are really dangerous operators. It might sound a bit dramatic using the phrase 'dangerous', but I really think that's the case. They have an influence on some young people's professional sports career and they exploit it for their own benefit. It means their decision making is skewed by what is right for them or will make them look good. The easiest example I can give of this is in cricket, with the Indian Premier League. The IPL is the richest and most high-profile franchised-based cricket competition in the world. If a cricketer goes there and does well, they will become an overnight superstar and millionaire. It really is that simple. However, the IPL comes with its potential pitfalls for young cricketers, and agents have to advise properly if they want to give their young client the best advice they can. This comes in two ways: monetarily, and what's right for their career.

English cricketers are fined a percentage of their wages for England, or with their county if not centrally contracted, for being at the IPL. This means that if they get picked up in the IPL draft for one of the lower reserve prices then they can actually make zero money for going to the tournament. Once the fine, agent's fee and tax are taken off, there can be nothing left for the player. Some players, Sam Billings being a good example, have done this willingly in order to gain the experience and exposure that the tournament provides. But there are other players who end up going to the IPL, and this takes them by surprise. This is made worse if they get picked up in the draft but then don't actually get selected for the starting line-up for their franchise. Their wages get cut to 80 per cent per game if they are not selected, and they sit on the bench while there are other players at home playing for their counties and making a case to be selected for England. Within all of this, the agent still gets paid a commission of wages, so the player can end up with zero and playing very little cricket, but the agent still gets paid. Agents who are driven by self-interest will not consider all these permutations as they should do, and will not explain this to their clients. Sadly, this happens.

I manage the very exciting cricketer Tom Moores, who, in my opinion, will make a huge impact in international and franchise-based cricket throughout his career. In his breakthrough year, he attracted attention from the franchise-based tournaments and, indeed, played in the T10 and Pakistan Super League tournaments. We discussed whether he should enter the 2019 IPL draft and although it was unlikely that he would get picked up, I still advised him not to enter. It wasn't the right time for him to go there. His game still needed to develop significantly, and he needed more time at the start of the English season at Nottinghamshire CCC. It could also set him adrift from his Nottinghamshire squad because they would be playing together while he was away in India. He would unintentionally become a bit of an outlier to the squad. He didn't need this to happen just yet in his career, plus he wouldn't make any money in the IPL because his only chance was to get picked up for a small amount at this stage in his career. I had to see what was best for him and advise accordingly. This should always happen with agents, but unfortunately, it doesn't.

Agents acting in self-interest also make decisions based on short-term gain, not for the long-term benefit of the client. This is worst reflected in what commercial deals they push their clients into. A young superstar in the making is often much better waiting for the big commercial offers they will get as they develop rather than going for a relatively poor offer early on in their career. Once a client is heavily associated with a brand then it can put off other brands from wanting to form a partnership, especially competing brands ... so you'd best make sure that original deal was worth it! Sometimes our job is as much about telling a client what not to do than telling them what to do. Remember my tale earlier on in the book about Paul Pogba and his boot deal? An agent acting predominantly in self-interest is not going to stay patient; they will want their money as quickly as possible, regardless of whether it works for the client in the long term.

Sam Quek was desperate to prove her worth as a sports presenter when she stepped away from hockey after the 2016 Rio Olympics. She is a very attractive woman and was offered lingerie endorsement deals that were worth a lot of money. She was resolute that she didn't want to do this sort of thing so that she could instead focus people on her broadcasting work, which is absolutely the right thing to do. And I have always backed that up for her, despite the quick money a deal like that might make for me.

Football is rife with stories that an agent perhaps pushed a player to go to a certain club because the agent's fee on offer was bigger at that particular club. This is true as many times as it is false. It is sometimes used as an excuse as to why a club can't sign a player, but it can also be a fact. It will exist as long as there is so much money in football and is the reason why young players have to be very careful who they sign with.

A client has to feel that you have their back. That comes in the form of you being smart and hard-working for them, but also that you are always looking at what is best for them in the long run and advise accordingly. If you don't act like that, then you will soon get found out, but sadly, agents like that don't really care. They are in and out for a quick buck and then move on to the next set of clients. That is why you must always look for agents who have a stable group of clients if you are looking for the best. They will be doing a lot of right things and always giving advice based on what is right for their clients in the long term.

If an agent is willing to take a chunk of the credit when their client does well, then they should also take an equal amount of criticism when things are not going well. Normally, that type of agent doesn't want it both ways, though. If you were to hire a lawyer or accountant to look after you, you would take every precaution to make sure you hired a person who would do everything they could to help you. Bringing an agent on board is no different, and why young sportspeople and their families should take their time in choosing an agent.

Afterword

Sometimes it seems like everything has changed in the sports industry over the last ten years – tactics, styles, competition formats, technology, clothing, sponsorship, earnings, broadcasters, fan bases … the list goes on and on.

But the importance and need of the sports agent hasn't changed.

In fact, there has actually been a significant rise in the role of the agent over this period. The sports industry needs the fluidity that agents provide more than ever. It needs its middleman to bridge the gap between many different parties who ultimately don't want to fall out. It means agents might always be the industry's punching bag, and always be tarred with that negative connotation about their role, but that's OK. If you choose to be a sports agent, then you have to understand the territory you're working in.

Cricket is a great example to illustrate the rise of the agent during the last decade. When I first started managing Jimmy Anderson, there was a maximum of four other agents who, between us, managed the players who stretched over the England squads. We used to have a meeting each year with the Director of Cricket (or equivalent role) and Commercial Director at the ECB to discuss all the relevant issues for the England players. It would generally be over a very pleasant pub lunch. There might have been a handful of other agents operating, but not with any real significance.

There are now approaching fifty ECB registered agents, and they are all busy! Cricket has changed enormously over the last few years, with new formats, new competitions and a different perspective on what is an 'international cricketer'. The days of the stereotypical high-earning international cricketer only looking like Alastair Cook or Jimmy Anderson have gone. There are now players doing extremely well on the Twenty 20 tournament circuit and have never played an international match. Earnings have skyrocketed and the landscape is unrecognisable from how it was in the early 2000s. In the middle of it all is the agent. And this is simply fulfilling the demand for the services an agent can provide.

The changes that have come to cricket are because the game has evolved to stay in the highly competitive race to win fans' attention. Growing fan bases or, crucially, keeping fans has never been harder for sports. And why does it matter? Because sponsorship and broadcasting rights value go hand in hand with it; and that money contributes enormously to the survival and growth of that sport. If you stand still, you fall behind, with possible dangerous consequences for the sport.

Cricket is not alone in this evolution. Almost all sports are doing something to adapt to the new age of sports broadcasting and winning audiences, and, guess what? With that comes an increasing role for the agent. There was a time when sports beyond the mainstream had few or zero agents operating in it. That's not the case anymore. If you are an aspiring sports agent, then there are opportunities everywhere.

I will finish with this …

Being a sports agent can be brutal. Brutally brilliant and brutally crap.

You are let inside the world of sporting geniuses, which is a privilege afforded to few. You get to see the nuts and bolts of how elite sport works around the world, and it is fascinating, challenging and never-ending. Ultimately, you are inside a world that others dream of.

But with this comes not such good stuff. You can be blamed when it is not your fault. You are often dealing with conflict. You are always on call. The highs are beautiful, but the lows can be very dark.

In spite of all this, I wouldn't change a thing. My job is a brilliant thing to do, so I do understand why others can be so fascinated by it.

Acknowledgements

Jonathan Wright – thank you for believing in me as an author and giving me the opportunity to now write my second book. You have made this all possible.

Sam Quek, Jimmy Anderson, Nile Wilson and James Taylor – thank you for being fantastic clients and, more importantly, friends; and for supporting me with this book.

All my previous clients – I am really grateful for the time I had working with you. It was all part of the journey that created some brilliant memories.

Activate Management – the business has had lots of different people work for it over the years so thank you to you all for your contributions and support.

Fellow agents – keep up the good fight! Let's fill the sports industry with hard-working, ethical and creative agents.